Watercolour Painting
Step-by-Step

SEARCH PRESS

Watercolour Painting Step-by-Step

Jackie Barrass · Richard Bolton · Ray Campbell Smith
Frank Halliday · William Newton · Wendy Tait
Bryan A. Thatcher

This version first published in Great Britain 2009

Search Press Limited
Wellwood, North Farm Road, Tunbridge Wells, Kent TN2 3DR

Reprinted 2010, 2011 (twice), 2014, 2016

Based on the following books published by Search Press:
Creative Watercolour Techniques by Richard Bolton, 2000
Flowers in Watercolour by Wendy Tait, 1999
Landscapes in Watercolour by Ray Campbell Smith, 2000
Laying a Watercolour Wash by Frank Halliday, 1999
Light in Watercolour by Jackie Barrass, 2000
Painting with Watercolours by William Newton, 1999
Wet-into-Wet by Bryan A. Thatcher, 1995

Originally published in 2001 as *Working With Watercolour*

Text copyright © Search Press Limited 2001, 2009
Photographs by Search Press Studios

Photographs and design copyright © Search Press Ltd 2001, 2009

ISBN: 978-1-84448-438-6

Suppliers
If you have difficulty in obtaining any of the materials and equipment mentioned in this book, then please visit the Search Press website for details of suppliers: www.searchpress.com

Publishers' note
All the step-by-step photographs in this book feature the authors demonstrating how to paint using watercolour. No models have been used.

Printed in Malaysia

Front cover
Chrysanthemums and Honesty
Jackie Barrass

Page 1
Overgrown Gateway
Richard Bolton

Pages 2–3
Sunset
William Newton

Page 5
Irises
Wendy Tait

Contents

Introduction

Nothing quite compares with the transparency, luminosity and sheer beauty of a well-painted watercolour. The medium has a wonderful flexibility which can accommodate many tastes, techniques and methods, and correctly applied, it comes close to capturing the glow and subtlety of nature itself.

The versatility of watercolour is an endless delight – you can create bright and bold effects, or soft, delicate areas of colour. You could lay in luminous washes and magical misty backgrounds, using them to create atmosphere in a simple landscape, or manipulate the mood of a painting by varying tonal values and the balance of colours used. With watercolour, you can be spontaneous, contrasting broad sweeps of colour with delicate detail, and dramatic brushstrokes with translucent washes. It is an exciting and challenging medium and one that is capable of many different methods of expression.

The seven authors contributing to this book all have their own ways of interpreting what they see. As tutors and experienced artists, they are aware of the many problems experienced by students, so the book is easy to follow, practical and informative. It is arranged so that you learn about all the materials used in watercolour, and about the colours and how to mix them, before progressing on to basic techniques such as laying washes, wet-into-wet, and dry-brush work. You can then learn about some of the exciting effects that can be produced using masking fluid, salt, backruns, spattering and sponging, before learning the basics of composition, perspective and the use of tone.

The authors explain in detail how to paint skies, trees and foliage, water and reflections, buildings and flowers. A series of step-by-step demonstrations show how all these subjects can be tackled, and each section is accompanied by a selection of inspirational paintings in a rich variety of styles.

This book is full of expert tips that will help watercolour enthusiasts, from the beginner to the experienced artist, to create fresh, glowing pictures. The seven authors featured show a wide variety of styles, and whichever you prefer, you will soon discover the joys of working with watercolour and delight in its freshness, immediacy and versatility.

Low Tide
Jackie Barrass
This painting shows how dramatic lighting effects can be captured in watercolour using vibrant colours. The fishing boats were backlit by a misty sun just emerging over the distant hills – giving a lovely golden glow to the pools of water. Atmospheric scenes like this are much favoured by watercolour artists.

Materials

Art suppliers hold vast ranges of materials, and it can be daunting for the beginner to decide what to buy. However, it is perfectly possible to create a beautiful painting with just one colour and one brush, so start with a few essentials and add more items as you become more addicted.

Paper

Watercolour paper is available in different sizes, surface finishes and weights (thicknesses). Always use good quality paper.

You can buy paper in sheet form, as spiral bound pads or in blocks. Sheets usually measure 760 x 560mm (30 x 22in), but pads and blocks are available in various sizes.

There are three standard types of surface finish: Hot Pressed (HP) has a smooth surface; NOT/Cold Pressed has a medium texture; and Rough has a heavy texture. However, surface finish does vary a great deal from make to make.

Watercolour paper is also made in a number of weights which range from 190gsm (90lb) up to 640gsm (300lb) or even more. The 190gsm paper is rather thin and would certainly require stretching (see page 20). The most widely used weight is 300gsm (140lb) and, if you use a quarter sheet 380 x 280mm (15 x 11in), it will not need stretching. For larger paintings, use a heavier paper.

It is useful to carry an A4 cartridge-paper sketch book with you when you go out, in which to make small sketches.

Paints

Watercolour paints are available in either pans or tubes. Some artists prefer tube paint because it is ready to use, it does not require wetting and it does not wear out your brushes so quickly. If you want to use pan colours, add a few drops of water to them from time to time to make sure they stay reasonably soft.

Paints also come in two grades – students' or artists' quality. Although artists' quality paints are more expensive, they are more brilliant and transparent, and produce stronger, more intense results. They also go further in the long run, so most artists consider them well worth the additional cost.

Art tutors recommend working with a limited palette to begin with – a narrow range of colours which you can get to know well. Avoid large, expensive paintboxes with dozens of different colours. A small one with plenty of mixing space is all you need.

Palette

There are lots of different palettes available. Plastic ones are light, cheap and easy to clean. Choose one with plenty of large compartments, for mixing washes. Your choice of colours can then be laid out in the small compartments. Some artists like to put them in a set order, so that they always know where they are when painting.

A portable palette is essential for outdoor work, but when working indoors, an old white china plate can be used.

Brushes

There is a wide variety of brushes available in different sizes and it is advisable to buy the best that you can afford. Pure sable brushes hold colour well, but you can also use blends of sable and ox-hair, or synthetic brushes. These are relatively inexpensive and make an excellent substitute.

It is better to buy a few brushes to begin with. There is a variation in the shape of heads, but the most useful basic brushes are called **rounds** and **flats**.

Rounds are completely round with pointed ends. They are available in a variety of sizes and are extremely versatile. They hold a great deal of paint when wet, have tapered points for fine lines and detail, and are probably the most commonly used among watercolourists.

Flats are broad, square, chisel-shaped. They can be used for damping down paper, applying larger washes and general blocking in.

There are other more specialist brushes available: **hakes** are wider than flats and are used for applying washes. **Riggers** are long-haired round brushes which are superb for painting the rigging on ships (hence the name rigger), and for all fine detail. **Wash** brushes are used for washing in large areas of colour, but some artists prefer to use a large round, or a flat brush.

As a guide, you should buy brushes suited to the scale and style of your painting. To start with, you will need at least one large brush for dealing with broad areas such as skies. A 25mm (1in) flat would be fine. In addition, you should have at least three rounds – Nos. 5, 10, 12 and 14 for general work, and most essentially, a No.1, 3 or 4 rigger for fine detail.

Note It is the publishers' custom to recommend synthetic materials as substitutes for animal products wherever possible. There are now a large number of brushes available made from artificial fibres and they are satisfactory substitutes for those made from natural fibres.

William Newton used a flat brush to wash in the sky in this painting.

A No. 10 round brush was used to block in the hull of the boat.

Fishing Boat
William Newton

The finished painting. The tip of a rigger brush was used to paint in the rigging of the boat.

Other materials

Water container Jam jars or old margarine tubs make adequate water containers.

Pencil A soft 2B pencil is ideal for sketching. You could use a B or HB, but harder leads can scratch the paper and leave unsightly marks.

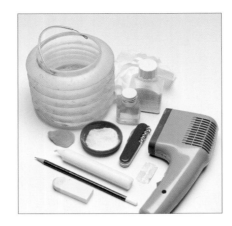

Eraser Use a soft eraser to remove pencil lines, and to create highlights on a painted surface.

Penknife or craft knife For sharpening pencils and cutting the finished painting from the painting board. It can also be used for the scratching-out technique.

Paper tissue This is ideal for cleaning your palette and for removing excess water from the brush. It can also be used for dabbing the painted surface to lift out unwanted colour.

Hairdryer Use this to speed up the drying process, but watch out for the formation of hard edges.

Sponge Use this for lifting out paint, and for creating large highlights.

Razor blade For scratching out fine lines such as blades of grass and twigs. It can also be used with an eraser to create highlights.

Candle For rubbing a wax resist on the paper prior to painting. The wax causes the paint to bead up and develop textural effects.

Ox gall This is a wetting agent that can be used in washes to help colours flow more freely. You can also use it to add highlights and unusual effects in washes – dabbed into the surface of a wet wash it will cause the colours to disperse from the point of application. It can be purchased in liquid or solid form.

Masking fluid Use this with an old brush for masking out intricate areas that would be hard to paint around.

Salt Sprinkle salt on wet paint to create abstract patterns and textures.

Rocky Riverbed
Richard Bolton
The artist used masking fluid, spattered into the background, to help create the quality of strong sunlight breaking through the foliage in this painting. The rough texture on the foreground rocks was created by wrubbing the paper with a white candle prior to painting.

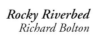

Painting boards and easels

Some watercolour artists like to work on a painting board alone, as this gives the freedom of movement to tip the painting to let the colour flow in certain directions. Boards can be plywood, blockboard or MDF. If you are using lightweight paper, you can pre-stretch it on the board before you begin painting (see page 20). If you have several boards, you will always have pre-stretched paper ready for painting.

   Other artists prefer to use an easel as well. There is a wide variety of easels available in wood or aluminium. A lightweight sketching easel is the most portable, and is useful for studio or outdoor work.

Equipment for painting outdoors

When painting outdoors, there are a number of items that you might need, such as a screw-topped jar for water, and an art case for spare paper. A light folding stool is ideal if you like to work seated. A groundsheet can be spread underneath you to keep the damp away, and it will also help you to spot things if you drop them. A flask of something to drink is of course always welcome!

A lightweight sketching easel can be used in the studio or outdoors.

Jackie Barrass uses a large plywood board when working outside. It is propped up to give a sloping surface while she is painting.

Colour

Colour is light. The spectrum shows us that white light contains all colours. An object will reflect some wavelengths and absorb others – the reflected light is the local, or true colour, of that object.

It is not possible to tell if each of us sees colours the same way, so our reaction to them is unique; it may be influenced by memories that trigger an emotional response. With this in mind, it is clear that colour can be a powerful and stimulating tool for self-expression.

Some painters prefer to rely on the use of tone in their paintings – colour is secondary to light and shade. Colourists, on the other hand, incorporate colour values and the interaction of colours into every stage of their painting process.

Whichever way you perceive colour in the world around you, one point that needs stressing is that the use of colours and tones must relate to those surrounding them. Therefore, try to maintain momentum over the whole painting surface, and you will achieve a sense of harmony. Do not restrict yourself by working on one area at a time.

When trying to analyse colour in your composition, it is useful to remember these characteristics.

Hue The name of a colour – red, blue, yellow etc. – irrespective of its tone or intensity.

Tone The relative lightness or darkness of a colour independent of its hue. Cadmium lemon, for example, is light in tone whilst cadmium yellow is relatively dark.

Intensity The brightness of a colour. Some colours, such as cadmium red, are really vibrant and can dominate surrounding colours, whereas light red is an earthy, duller red with less intensity. The intensity of colours can be reduced by adding, say, a complementary colour of similar tone.

Temperature The closeness of a colour to the warm (red/yellow) or cool (blue/green) parts of the spectrum. However, 'warm' hues can also vary in temperature. Cadmium red is considered as a warm red, while permanent rose is much cooler. Similarly, pthalo blue is relatively cooler in temperature than French ultramarine.

Canal Bridge
Jackie Barrass
The subtle mood of this painting is achieved by mixing colours such as the muted greys and soft pinky mauves. Intense colours would detract from this mellow composition.

Mixing colours

Each artist uses a different range of colours. You can study the vast range of books explaining colour theory, but the only effective way to learn about colour and paint is to have a go. Whilst you can use just one of each primary colour (red, blue and yellow), it is best to start your palette off with two basic reds, blues and yellows (one from each end of the temperature scale); you can mix your greens, oranges and violets (secondary colours) from these. Spend some time making your own colour wheel from the primary colours. Test the physical properties of the watercolour pigments and build up your own bank of knowledge so that using and mixing colours becomes second nature. Get to know how a small selection of pigments react with each other before introducing further colours to your palette. Some artists avoid black, neutral tints and Payne's gray, preferring to obtain dark colours by mixing primary colours together.

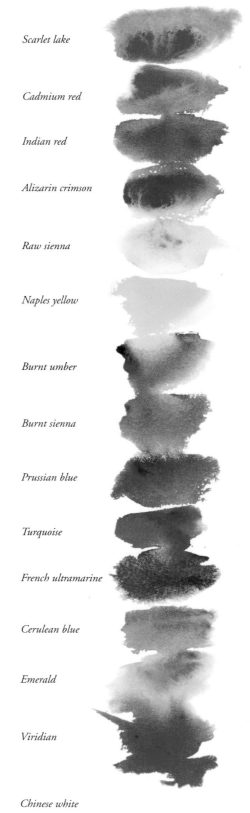

Scarlet lake

Cadmium red

Indian red

Alizarin crimson

Raw sienna

Naples yellow

Burnt umber

Burnt sienna

Prussian blue

Turquoise

French ultramarine

Cerulean blue

Emerald

Viridian

Chinese white

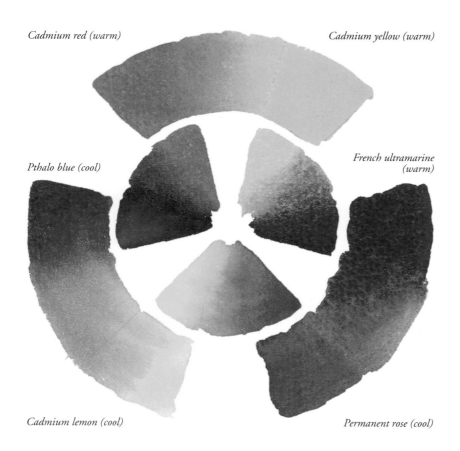

Cadmium red (warm)

Cadmium yellow (warm)

Pthalo blue (cool)

French ultramarine (warm)

Cadmium lemon (cool)

Permanent rose (cool)

Jackie Barrass's colour wheel (above) uses two of each primary colour – one warm and one cool tone. From these Jackie mixes a large range of colours, but she limits herself to six or seven in any one painting, to create a sense of unity.

Richard Bolton uses a standard set of fifteen colours (right), to which he occasionally adds special colours.

Using a limited palette

Most artists develop their own palette of preferred colours over time. William Newton, who painted the scene below, uses a palette of twelve colours that has evolved over years of experimentation. The painting shows how many different shades and tones can be created by mixing colours and diluting them with clean water.

If you haven't yet gained the confidence to develop your own palette, you can begin by adopting the range of colours of an artist with whose work and style you are in sympathy.

You should aim at being able to create exactly the right colours and tones you need for a particular subject, first time round, without too much correcting. This way you are much more likely to produce clean, fresh and transparent paintings. So, the rule is practice, practice and more practice!

William Newton uses French ultramarine, light red and raw sienna in most of his paintings, and his full palette also includes Cerulean blue, Winsor blue, cobalt blue, brown madder, burnt umber, burnt sienna, lemon yellow, cadmium red and cadmium yellow. The painting below is annotated to show how colours were chosen and mixed to achieve the desired shades.

French ultramarine and raw sienna

Cobalt blue wash

Cadmium red and raw sienna

Cerulean blue and light red

French ultramarine, raw sienna and cadmium yellow

Raw sienna

Cadmium red

Burnt sienna

Cadmium red

Burnt umber

Colours for flowers

Different selections of colours are required for different purposes. Wendy Tait's palette, shown here, is used for flower painting. The colours are listed (right), and Wendy always squeezes them out in the same order. She uses two Winsor lemons, one to keep pure and the other to mix with Payne's gray to make a basic green. Most artists advise against using green straight from a tube or pan, as it can look very artificial. The palette also includes two cobalt blue deeps, one to keep pure, the other to mix from. Winsor orange is the only semi-opaque colour used, since watercolour artists prefer transparent colours, which allow the paper to shine through pale washes.

Cobalt blue deep
Ultramarine violet
Winsor violet
Brown madder
Winsor orange
Quinacridone magenta
Scarlet lake
Permanent rose
Quinacridone gold
Raw umber
Raw sienna
New gamboge
Payne's gray
Winsor lemon

Wendy Tait's painting combines both warm and cool colours – pinks, violets and a warm golden background give it a glow, and the light greens are used to balance the effect.

18

Colours for landscapes

The paintbox shown on the right belongs to the landscape artist, Ray Campbell Smith, who uses raw sienna, burnt sienna, light red, French ultramarine, Winsor blue and Payne's gray. Sometimes he adds alizarin crimson and the umbers, while for sunnier landscapes he includes cadmium yellow and cadmium orange.

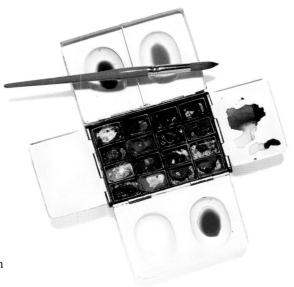

Ray uses raw sienna mixed with a touch of Winsor blue for painting meadow grass, while for a brighter green (perhaps for the lusher grass of garden lawns), he uses cadmium yellow, instead of raw sienna. For dry grass or hay, he finds that raw sienna with a little French ultramarine is about right. If you prefer to use a ready-made green, olive green is about the most natural for grass and foliage, but even this usually needs a little added yellow.

Cadaques, Catalonia
Ray Campbell Smith
A bright palette is used to capture the colours of this Mediterranean scene.

Techniques

This section shows you how to stretch a lightweight paper before painting. It also introduces you to four types of wash – flat, graded, variegated and broken, and how to use them, and to the basic techniques of watercolour.

Stretching paper

Before you can begin to paint, you need to decide which paper you want to work on. Some artists prefer heavyweight papers – more than 425gsm (200lb) – which do not require stretching. If you choose a lightweight paper (see page 8), it will require stretching to prevent it from distorting when a wet wash is applied. Although this may sound complicated, the technique is not difficult, and it is essential if you want to create even washes. If you are a prolific artist, it is a good idea to stretch several pieces of paper at a time on extra pieces of board.

Note It is advisable to stretch paper twenty-four hours before you need it, to allow time for it to dry completely. Alternatively, use a hairdryer to speed up drying time.

1. Immerse the paper in a bowl of cold water for approximately three minutes.

2. Remove the paper carefully. Allow excess water to drain off, then place it centrally on a board.

3. Tear four strips of gummed paper to fit around the edges of the paper. Wet the strips and use them to secure the paper to the board – place each strip approximately 20mm (in) over the edge of the paper.

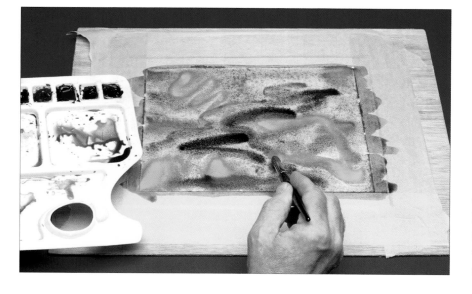

4. Allow the paper to dry, keeping the board flat. You are now ready to paint, and however wet your washes are, the paper should remain taut.

Laying washes

Washes are simple and extremely effective. They can be used to create different effects – from soft skies and misty landscapes, to dense foliage and dramatic seas. Depending on the paper you use, you may need to wet the paper before you lay the wash – this will ensure that the wash is even. It is advisable to practise the technique first.

Flat washes are best laid in on dry paper, but they can also be worked on a wet surface. The varying degrees of wetness on the paper will affect the evenness of the wash.

Graded washes are ideal for creating the effect of distance in a landscape, for example. If you use a strong wash at the top, and weaken it down gradually as you come towards the horizon, you will create a three-dimensional effect.

Variegated washes are created using two or more colours. The different colours will fuse into each other where they meet on the paper to create wonderful effects. If you are really pleased with a particular variegated wash, make a note of the colours used so you can reproduce it again in the future.

A **broken wash** is useful if you are painting an area that has a somewhat rough surface, such as a field of hay. The technique naturally works better on Rough paper.

Note It is advisable to choose a large brush when working a wash, as this will hold the most liquid, distribute the colour evenly, and ensure that the wash remains fluid.

Use a scrap piece of paper, similar to the one you are going to paint on, to test the suitability and strength of colour.

For all washes, it is best to work on a sloping board. Mix sufficient colour in advance, to cover your paper – this is important as it is impossible to recreate a mix exactly if you run out.

Flat wash

1. Load a No. 12 round brush with diluted colour. Lay in an even stroke along the top of the paper. While still wet, slightly overlap a second stroke over the first. Continue until you have completed the wash.

2. When you get to the end of the wash, dry the brush on paper tissue, then use it to soak up excess paint.

Graded wash

1. Use a No. 12 round brush to lay in several strokes of colour along the top of the paper.

2. Gradually add water to the colour to weaken it. Continue to lay in strokes, adding water as you go, to complete the wash.

Variegated wash

1. Lay in a few strokes of your first colour along the top of the paper, then lay in a stroke of the second colour as shown.

2. Continue working several strokes of the second colour, then introduce a third colour.

Broken wash

First prepare a pool of colour and then apply it with swift, horizontal strokes of a large brush held almost parallel to the paper. The brush should skate over the surface, leaving chains of white dots where it has missed the little depressions in the rough finish.

Wet-into-wet

The essence of watercolour is its transparency and fluidity, and the technique of painting wet-into-wet, which means painting on a surface which is already wet, really brings out these qualities. You can achieve some wonderful flowing effects for skies, landscapes, water, trees and a host of other subjects, simply by controlling and experimenting with your washes of colour.

To make it all look so effortless, you will have to put in a bit of practice, of course, but this sort of experimenting is always fun.

The most important thing is to understand the effects of the degree of wetness of the paint on both the brush and the paper.

The four illustrations below indicate the results of various degrees of wetness. You will see that the wet-into-wet example has fused the colours together in a most attractive manner. The damp-into-damp and the damp-into-wet examples have also worked quite well. In the last example, though, the wet brush placing wet colour into a previously applied damp colour has resulted in an unattractive drying stain.

The wet-into-wet technique requires practice, but can produce fluid, transparent results, as shown in the above sketch.

It is well worth remembering that wet-into-damp usually results in disasters, so do plan your painting so that the second colour is ready to use before the first has dried out. When your work becomes more advanced, there may be occasions when this technique can be used to create some special effects, but for now be wary of using it.

The wet-into-wet technique is rewarding when laying down an initial wash: it can give a painting lots of 'atmosphere'. Use blues and greys for cool distant backgrounds, or add a little red to give a touch of warmth to your background.

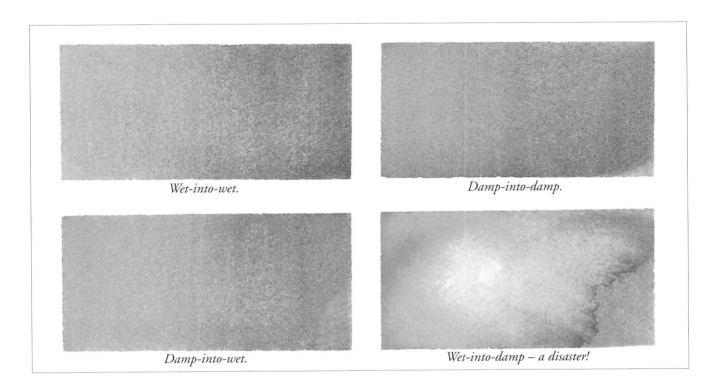

Wet-into-wet.

Damp-into-damp.

Damp-into-wet.

Wet-into-damp – a disaster!

Apply a generous amount of light red and allow the paint to run into the wetted paper.

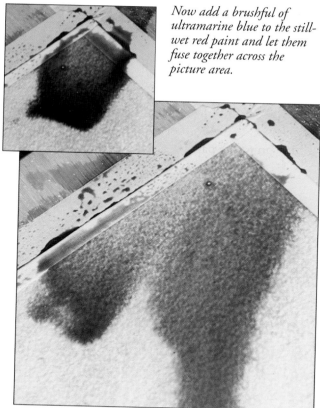

Now add a brushful of ultramarine blue to the still-wet red paint and let them fuse together across the picture area.

Laying a wet-into-wet two-colour wash

The illustrations on this page show how exciting the fusing of one colour into another can be. First the whole area to be painted was wetted with a generous amount of clean water. Then light red was applied to the top corner of the paper and allowed to run into the wetted area. Then another brush was loaded with ultramarine blue and this was allowed to run into the wet red. You must paint fairly quickly to ensure that the first wash is still wet when the second colour is added, so ensure that both colours are mixed in the palette before starting the first wash.

People often fail to mix enough colour in the palette. It is far better to mix more than you need than to run out of colour. If you do run out and have to mix more, you may find that the paint on the paper has already dried out too much. A second colour will not fuse properly with a dried-out first colour.

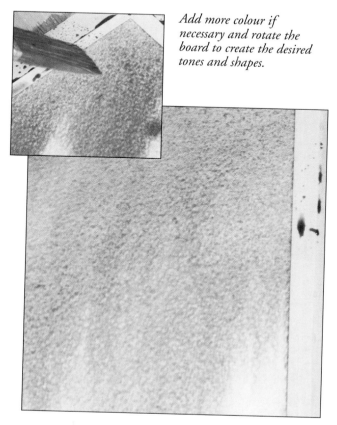

Add more colour if necessary and rotate the board to create the desired tones and shapes.

24

Dry-brush work

For this technique you need to use as little water as possible. The paint sits on the textured surface of the paper (rather than soaking into it) to leave speckles of white paper amidst the brush strokes. There is a fine line between not having enough water in the brush and too much, so experiment with the technique on a piece of scrap paper.

Dry-brush work is very hard on brushes – they have to be pressed firmly on to the paper – so select an old brush that has lost its point.

Load a brush with colour, then soak up excess water, without removing the paint, by touching a paper tissue against the hairs of the brush where they meet the ferrule.

The paint breaks up as the brush is dragged across the surface of the paper. These marks could be the speckled highlights on a river.

Dry-brush work was used to create the rugged surface of this pot.

Here, random scrubbing of colour gives the texture of grassy undergrowth.

In this scene by Richard Bolton, dry-brush work has been used extensively to render the ragged canopy of shade under the large tree.

Splayed brush

This is another technique that comes in useful, particularly when painting landscapes. The brush head is pinched at the point where the hairs enter the ferrule. This causes the hairs to fan out so that, when loaded with pigment, they may be used to paint clumps of foreground grass or reeds. It is a method that should be used with restraint, or a repetitive fringe-effect may result.

Blocking in

Blocking in is a simple matter of filling areas of the paper with colour which can then be glazed over with other colours to add shape and form. Flat brushes are eminently suitable for working this technique.

Overlaid glazing

You can use the transparent quality of watercolours to create medium and darker tones simply by glazing a second layer of wash over a dry first layer. However, you must work briskly, yet lightly, so as not to disturb the first wash. This technique is especially useful when painting shadows.

Fine lines

A rigger can be used for most fine lines. The original use for this brush was, as its name suggests, for painting the rigging on boats in marine pictures. However, in landscapes, it is especially useful for painting tapering branches and twigs on trees. The brush is usually held upright and line thickness is changed by varying the downward pressure. Work a tapered line from the thick end out to the fine tip.

Morning Glory
William Newton
Fine lines like the rigging on the boats in this picture are usually painted with a rigger brush.

Other techniques

Masking fluid This is very effective for masking out intricate areas that would be hard to paint around, especially when applying a wash, where speed is essential. To remove it, simply rub it away with a soft eraser.

Scratching out This technique is useful for creating the fine lines of a tangle of undergrowth, or for graining a piece of wood. Wait until the paint is nearly dry and then scratch out the lines with a sharp penknife or razor blade.

Wax resist When a candle is rubbed on the paper, it forms a resist that causes the paint to bead. It is useful for creating textured areas on rocks or tree bark. An effective but unpredictable technique.

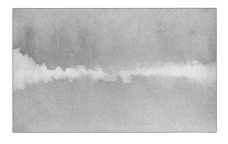

Ox gall This is a wetting agent that helps washes run more smoothly. It is useful for painting wet-into-wet effects; the paint tends to flow away from the point of application and create unusual patterns.

Salt Salt sprinkled over a wet surface can have a spectacular effect. As the salt dissolves, a speckle of white dots develop. Its effects are rather unpredictable, and are best used in free-flowing, imaginative washes.

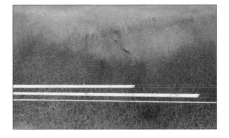

Cutting out Very effective for creating fine white highlights, such as in river scenes where a fine shaft of light cuts across the water. Cut two lines close together, then carefully scratch away the strip between the cuts.

Rubbing out A useful way of adding gentle highlights. Simply rub away with an eraser. You can use it against the edge of a ruler to give a straight line of highlight.

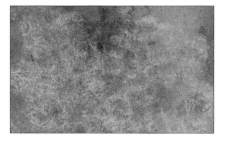

Dabbing Dark areas of colour can be made more interesting by dabbing them with a sponge or paper tissue. However, take care not to create a muddy mix.

Split brush This technique is very useful for developing foliage. Press a brush into the palette to splay out its bristles, then dab the paint on to the paper.

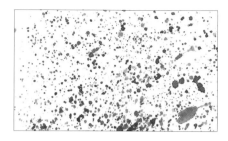

Spattering Tap a loaded brush against a finger so that a spatter of fine dots of paint fall on the paper. Cover the area you do not want spattered, as the dots of paint can travel a long way. Alternatively, use the technique with masking fluid to create speckled highlights.

Sponging The sponge can be an all-purpose tool. Some artists use it a lot for painting cloud effects. Others use it for lifting out large areas of paint, especially for big soft-edged highlights on water.

Imprinting Paint can be picked up and transferred to the painting by way of dabbing with a sponge or tissue to add textural qualities.

Overpainting This technique (using opaque colours) must be applied sensitively to work well – if opaque colours are worked indiscriminately, the wonderful quality of watercolour will be lost. Here Richard Bolton uses two opaque colours, Naples yellow and Chinese white, which he mixes with the transparent colours. Overpainting is very useful for areas of foliage and grass, where the delicate tapestry of leaves can be suggested by stippling with a fine brush. For larger areas, overpainting with the split-brush technique can be very effective.

A little overpainting can work wonders with brickwork.

The quality of foliage can be built up using the split-brush technique.

Positive and negative

This technique is also known as 'push and pull'. When painting a well-lit object, you should lay down the initial wash, let it dry and then simply paint the darker area around your lit subject matter to bring it into focus. Work in reverse for dark objects seen against a well-lit background. This sounds like an obvious technique but it is often overlooked.

Softening

After carefully wetting a selected area you can use a cotton bud or soft brush to blend or merge unwanted hard edges. Small, soft highlights can also be lifted out in this way. Be aware that certain pigments stain the paper, making it impossible to get back to a really white surface. In addition, some papers hold on to pigment more than others.

Backruns

Backruns look like accidents but they are used deliberately by many artists to great effect. Unplanned backruns can be a nuisance to a beginner and are only resolved by lifting out. They occur when fresh colour is applied to a wash before the previous layer is dry – the result is that the new paint creeps into the old. The unusual textures and edge qualities can, however, be incorporated into your painting.

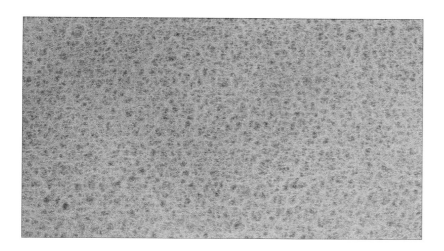

Granulation

When pigment settles out of a wash into the grain of the paper, it can produce lovely atmospheric speckles. This effect is known as granulation. It can add subtle interest to otherwise flat areas of paint. Certain pigments are prone to this effect (French ultramarine, for example) and some papers react better than others. Rough paper is particularly good to work on as it has an uneven surface.

Chrysanthemums and Honesty
Jackie Barrass
No masking fluid was used in this flower painting, but some highlights were lifted out using the softening technique.

Composition and Perspective

Composition

Planning and composition are essential to successful watercolour painting. In this context, composition simply means the arrangement of the elements of your chosen subject on the paper in such a way that the overall effect is pleasing and harmonious. This is not quite as easy as it sounds. There are a number of all too common faults you should be aware of if you are to achieve attractive and well-balanced compositions. Here are some ways of avoiding these common errors.

• Never cut your painting into two equal halves, either horizontally (perhaps by placing the horizon exactly half way up the paper), or vertically (by placing some dominant vertical such as a church spire too centrally). See the examples on page 34. Move the horizon down if the sky is an interesting one, or up, if you are more interested in the scene below. Move the dominant feature to the right or left and then balance it with some other feature.

• Avoid having all the tonal weight on one side of your painting – it can usually be balanced by placing a dark tree or heavy cloud on the other side. Be aware of this danger and then use your ingenuity!

• Try to include tonal contrasts – the placing of lights against darks and darks against lights. You can use a little artistic licence to achieve this, for instance, by moving a dark copse behind a group of pale-toned cottages.

• It is always a good plan to have a focal point or a centre of interest in your painting, a point to which the eye is naturally drawn. If you can arrange some of the main construction lines of your composition so that they help to lead the eye to this focal point, so much the better. Avoid having two competing focal points – the eye will move from one to the other and find nowhere to come to rest.

Castle on Headland
Ray Campbell Smith

Here the tonal weight of the castle on its promontory is balanced by the heavy cloud on the right and its reflection.

Wealden Farm in Winter
Ray Campbell Smith

The farmer and his dog provide human interest as well as a focal point. The line of the farm track carries the eye towards them and the shape of the foreground snowy roof points directly at them.

- If your composition includes any moving objects, such as horse riders or sailing boats, make sure you have them moving into your painting rather than out of it, so that the eye of the beholder is also drawn into the heart of your painting.

- Features such as roads, tracks, rivers and streams can easily carry the eye straight out of the painting. In these instances, it often pays to use a building, a group of trees, or some other object as a blocking device.

- Avoid what is sometimes referred to as the 'coincidence of unrelated lines'. For example, if the roof line of a foreground building is exactly in line with the horizon, correct it by either raising or lowering the offending roof.

33

Rule of thirds

In simple terms, this means that the horizon and focal point are better placed somewhat off-centre. The horizon line should be approximately one-third up from the bottom (or one-third down from the top) of a picture, and the main focal point or element within the composition should also be placed one-third in from one side. This is all good advice but, like all rules, it can be broken occasionally.

These two paintings by William Newton show how you can improve a composition by adjusting the positions of the horizon and focal point.

In the composition above, the farm buildings are placed in the centre of the painting, and the large tree appears to cut the image in half. The centred horizon leaves a large expanse of uninteresting foreground.

Although the painting shown right was painted from the same viewpoint as the one above, this version has a well-balanced composition. The focal point is offset to the right and the horizon is roughly one-third up from the bottom. The introduction of deep shadows in the foreground helps draw the eye into the painting.

Avoiding faults is a necessary if rather negative process. A more positive approach is to study the paintings of accomplished artists and work out for yourself why you find their compositions pleasing and attractive.

Perspective

The most difficult aspect of painting is interpreting what we see. Most of what we observe is an illusion caused by distance. Linear and aerial perspective are used to help recreate this illusion on paper.

Linear perspective

Physical objects such as buildings and roads do not really taper to a vanishing point, nor do they get smaller in size with distance, they only appear to. This illusion is referred to as linear perspective, and in general terms it means that all parallel lines converge to a point on the horizon. Remember that the horizon must always be at your eye level. The way in which the lines taper depends on your viewpoint relative to the horizon.

These small sketches are included to illustrate the principles of linear perspective.

Aerial perspective

Distance also affects our visual perception of colour, tones and contrasts. As an object recedes into the distance, its colour appears to fade, and this is known as aerial perspective. The trick is to observe these effects carefully and to develop the skill to represent them in a way that is both stimulating and pleasing to the eye. This is a technique that can be exploited (and exaggerated) to make truly three-dimensional images.

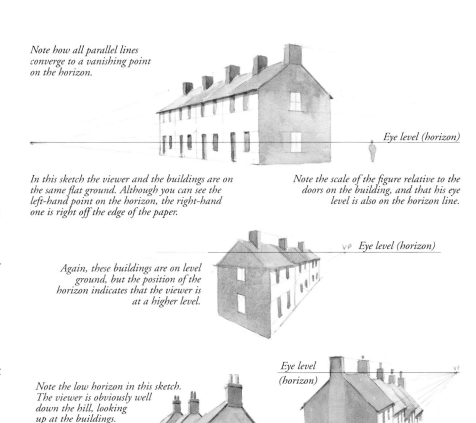

Note how all parallel lines converge to a vanishing point on the horizon.

Eye level (horizon)

In this sketch the viewer and the buildings are on the same flat ground. Although you can see the left-hand point on the horizon, the right-hand one is right off the edge of the paper.

Note the scale of the figure relative to the doors on the building, and that his eye level is also on the horizon line.

VP Eye level (horizon)

Again, these buildings are on level ground, but the position of the horizon indicates that the viewer is at a higher level.

Eye level (horizon)

Note the low horizon in this sketch. The viewer is obviously well down the hill, looking up at the buildings.

Eye level (horizon)

The high horizon in this sketch indicates that the viewer is standing at a point level with the top of the roof of the nearest building.

This is a typical example of aerial perspective, where colours and tones become cooler as they recede into the distance.

Understanding Tone

The variation of tonal value, in terms of the dark and light areas of a subject, is an important aspect of any painting. One way of appreciating tone is to look at a scene through half-closed eyes – the more you close them, the greater is the contrast between light and dark. Painting in monochrome (using diluted shades of just one colour) helps you understand the importance of tone. Any colour can be used, but a dark colour which dilutes down to almost clear is best. Sepia is one such colour.

Farmhouse

This is a good subject for a monochrome painting as there is a strong source of light (coming from the left) that creates contrasting areas of light and dark. It also includes flat surfaces with different tonal values, a few trees silhouetted against a clear sky, and strong foreground shadows that give depth to the scene.

When painting with watercolours, whether in monochrome or a range of colours, try to work from top to bottom, from light to dark and from background to foreground. This demonstration by William Newton was painted on a 380 x 280mm (15 x 11in) sheet of 425gsm (200lb) Rough paper.

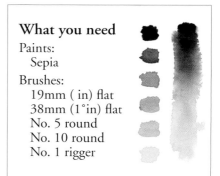

What you need

Paints:
  Sepia
Brushes:
  19mm (in) flat
  38mm (1°in) flat
  No. 5 round
  No. 10 round
  No. 1 rigger

Although it is best to do most of your painting on site, it's a good idea to make one or two pencil field sketches for future reference. You can use these to decide on composition, direction of light and the position and shape of shadows. You could also take a few photographs in case your activities are curtailed by unforeseen circumstances – a change in the weather or lighting, or even someone blocking your view with a large truck!

1. Fix the paper to the painting board and use the field sketch as a reference to lightly pencil in the outlines of the main elements of the picture. Then, use the 38mm (1°in) flat brush and clean water to wet all the paper except the farmhouse which, for the moment, is left dry.

3. Use a No. 5 round brush and a slightly darker tone of colour to paint the distant horizon. Add more colour, then paint the roof and chimneys, leaving highlights for the flashing. Use an even darker tone to paint the small bush in front of the farmhouse.

2. Use the 19mm (in) flat brush to lay a wash of diluted sepia over the wet areas. Apply stronger tones of colour towards the top and bottom of the picture to accentuate perspective. Leave to dry.

4. Now, working up from light to dark tones, use a No. 10 round brush to paint the foliage on the trees. Lightly drag the side of a loaded brush across the dry paper, allowing areas of the paper to show through. Use the same dry-brush technique to add the bushes at the base of the tree.

5. Use the rigger brush to paint the trunk and branches. Push the brush down on to the paper for the thicker part of each branch and then gradually lift it as the branch gets progressively thinner. Paint the left-hand tree in the same way.

6. Use the No. 5 brush to glaze a shadow over the left-hand roof, then paint the shadows on the walls and gable end of the farmhouse.

7. Paint the furrows that lead the eye into the painting, with a mid-tone. Use small touches of a darker tone to create light, shade and form in the trees and other features.

The finished painting. Broad strokes of a loaded No. 10 brush were used to lay in the foreground shadows. Some of the lighter undertones were allowed to peep through and create a feeling of dappled light over rough ground. Although the furrows naturally lead the eye into the picture, darkening the foreground emphasises the sunlit area in the centre of the painting and lifts the eye to it.

Fishing Boats
William Newton

This picture was painted in the same way as the demonstration opposite. Again, the light source is coming sharply from the left.

It might be fun to paint other studies using a different colour. Try burnt umber for a warm effect, or use a cool colour such a blue to create the impression of a night-time scene.

Note *If you do not like your first attempt at a painting, do another version of the same subject immediately afterwards, while any mistakes you made are still fresh in your mind.*

Monochrome study of a country church, by William Newton.

Skies

If you want to paint landscapes, you need to be competent at producing a number of different skies. The sky often provides the setting for a picture, and it should always be considered as part of the overall composition. The type of sky you paint rather depends on the subject, the kind of scene you are trying to represent, and the other elements that are to be included.

If the composition is high in content, with architecture, trees or boats providing strong verticals, and if it has plenty of middle distance and foreground interest, there is a good case for having a relatively simple sky. If, on the other hand, the focal points are distant and flat, then perhaps a low horizon and a dramatic cloud formation might be called for. In the following sketches by William Newton, the sky is a fairly dominant element of the picture.

Storm Clouds
This sky is painted wet on dry, with some areas of the paper left white to denote highlights.

Evening Sky
Here, the sky is painted wet-into-wet, with warm tones graded from the bottom to the top of the clouds.

Morning Mist

Again, this sky is painted wet-into-wet. Note the use of violet tones that are laid across the lower sky and into hills on the horizon.

Sunset

Hardly any blue has been used for this sky. Warm mixes of raw sienna and cadmium red are painted wet-into-wet. The setting sun is left dry at first, then a touch of dilute cadmium yellow is painted into it.

In a painting with a busy sky, like this one by Bryan Thatcher, it is best to keep the foreground quiet and simple.

The examples on this page and the one opposite were all painted by Bryan Thatcher, and they demonstrate some of the techniques and colour combinations that can be used.

Study the composition of clouds – the main types are listed on page 45. Clouds have shadows, usually underneath them when the source of light (the sun) is above them. When the sun is low on the horizon, the shadows will sometimes be on top of them.

Two useful sky washes: (left) ultramarine blue brushed into a wet light red; (right) a mixture of ultramarine blue and brown madder alizarin brushed into a wet Naples yellow.

A colourful hazy sky made from Naples yellow, light red, ultramarine blue and brown madder alizarin. Useful when a warm atmosphere is required.

This is a cooler sky but it still indicates some sunlight behind the hazy clouds. It is made from the same colours as the above example but with a little less light red and brown madder alizarin.

This is the type of sky seen most often. Cobalt blue and a little neutral tint make the grey areas, while the blue sky comes from just a little cobalt blue laid down on dry paper.

Lively skies

As you have already seen, freshness and translucence are of vital importance in watercolour painting and this applies with particular force to the treatment of skies. You should therefore do all you can to preserve these desirable qualities and aim to create an impression of light and movement. The old adage, plan like a tortoise, paint like a hare is worth remembering in this context!

The variegated wash is ideal for rendering cloudless skies. For this you must prepare two washes, one for the pale, warm tones just above the horizon and the other for the stronger blues higher up in the sky. You do not always have to match exactly the colours of nature and some of the more brilliant Mediterranean blues should be understated in the gentle medium of watercolour. At the same time you must remember that watercolour fades on drying and you should allow for this when mixing your washes.

When painting clouds, it is best to use washes which blend to produce soft edges, but you can also preserve a few hard edges for the sake of variety. The painting below by Ray Campbell Smith shows a sky painted in this manner. An alternative method of painting cloudy skies is to wet the whole of the sky area first, perhaps by applying a variegated wash, and then to drop in colours for the clouds, wet-into-wet. With this method, all the edges are soft, to produce a

Loch Long, Wester Ross
Ray Cambpell Smith

Eilean Donan Castle
Ray Campbell Smith

smooth, overall effect. The sky in the painting above was painted in this way. Notice how the light red has separated from the French ultramarine to give the clouds a warm halo. The level formations of stratus clouds give skies a settled, peaceful appearance and are useful if this is the message you want to convey in your painting. They may be painted with bold, horizontal strokes of a large brush, either wet on dry, if you want crisp edges, or wet-into-wet if you prefer a softer image.

Skies become more exciting from the artist's point of view when there are interesting cloud formations and here some knowledge of the main cloud types is helpful. With all types of cloud, observation and conscientious practice are the dual keys to success.

The four main categories are listed here, but there are also in-between formations, such as cumulo-nimbus and cirro-stratus.

- **Cirrus** These are the high altitude, fluffy, white clouds composed of frozen water vapour.

- **Stratus** As the name suggests, these clouds form smooth layers which can cover the whole sky or part of it.

- **Cumulus** These are the billowing clouds with high, domed crests and level bases.

- **Nimbus** These are the storm clouds, often heavy and dark in tone, with broken, ragged edges.

In any event, we need to make skies interesting – but do not overwork them.

Cumulus Clouds

Cumulus clouds are the most paintable of all. There is no need to draw the cloud outlines first, and most artists are happy to go straight in with the brush. At the same time, you should have some idea of the overall shapes, or you may unthinkingly end up with two or three clouds of almost the same shape and size.

Begin by preparing three washes: one for the warm tones lower in the sky, the second wash for the cloud shadows and the third wash for the blue of the sky. The order in which these washes are applied is a matter of personal choice. You could start with the pale wash for the lower sky. You can then dilute it for the areas of sunlit clouds, which go in next. Next put in the cloud shadows, to the undersides of the clouds and the sides away from the source of light, and finally apply the blue wash, which helps to delineate the upper shapes of the clouds.

1. Use a 25mm (1in) flat brush to apply a wash of raw sienna mixed with a touch of light red above the horizon. Dilute this colour with a lot of water and use this to paint in the sunlit area of the clouds. Use a wash of ultramarine and light red to paint in the cloud shadows. The grey of the cloud shadows tends to be warmer just above the horizon and cooler higher in the sky, so adjust the proportions of ultramarine and light red in your washes accordingly.

2. Use ultramarine with just a touch of light red for the blue of the sky.

Note As you are painting the sky, use a 12mm (°in) flat brush to soften some edges with water, but leave others hard.

3. Paint in the grass in the foreground using a No. 12 round brush and a broken wash of raw sienna with a touch of Winsor blue. Add texture using the same colour and a No. 6 brush.

4. Use a No. 10 round brush with raw and burnt sienna and Winsor blue in various proportions to paint in the tree. Add shadows with a No. 6 round brush, using a deeper mix of burnt sienna and Winsor blue.

5. Paint in the hedge using a No. 10 round brush and the same colours as in the previous step. Use a No. 6 round brush to add a little shadow underneath as you work. Remember to leave a gap for the gate.

6. Paint in the gate using a No. 6 round brush and a mix of burnt sienna and Winsor blue.

7. Add more shadows underneath the hedge using a No. 10 brush with a mix of burnt sienna and Winsor blue.

The finished painting

A wet-into-wet sky

This snow scene by Bryan Thatcher features a sky painted using the wet-into-wet technique to create a luminous effect.

One real advantage of painting snow scenes in watercolour is of course that we can use the white of the paper for the snow itself. The work is half completed before we begin!

Should you not wish to paint out on location in extremely cold conditions for long periods, why not produce one or two five-minute pencil sketches instead? These can be used as references back in the warmth and comfort of the studio. The camera can also be used, but do not be tempted to copy photographs too slavishly, as the limited range of tones within a photograph can be very misleading.

If you do decide to venture out, limit your materials to a minimum, but leave room for that vacuum flask of hot tea!

This demonstration takes you through all the stages of painting the scene depicted in the sketch (below), and explains how the artist used different brushes and various colour mixes to achieve the end result. You will note that in the finished picture he decided to include three figures rather than the two in the sketch.

Original sketch

1. Mix up thin washes of light red and cobalt blue. Wet the area of sky with clean water and then use the flat wash brush to add the light red.

2. Start to add the cobalt blue while the light red is still wet, beginning at the right-hand side of the picture.

3. Tilt the painting board to allow the cobalt blue to run away from the centre of the painting, leaving a light in the sky.

4. Now add cobalt blue to the left-hand side and tilt the board again to create a light area in the centre of the sky. When you are satisfied, put the picture on a flat surface to dry.

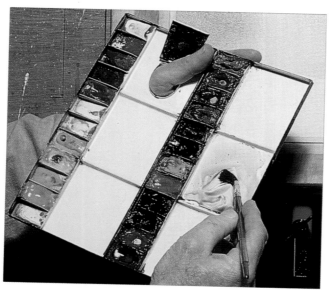

5. Mix a little brown madder alizarin with some cobalt blue: this colour is for the trees at the left-hand side of the picture.

6. Add a little of the mix to a flat chisel-edge brush and then paint on to the dried paper indicating foliage on the winter tree.

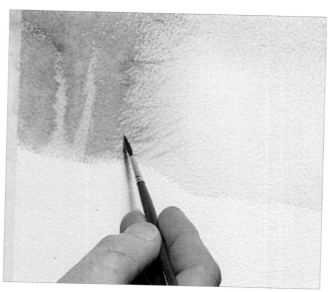

7. Change to a No. 4 round brush and using the same mixture flick on one or two suggestions of branches. Lay colour around the indications of the tree trunks.

8. Use a stronger mix of the same two colours to paint in the trees on the right of the picture. The brush should not be too wet: this will allow a dry-brush effect to leave lights appearing through the trees.

9. With a clean dry finger, push some of the colour off the edge of the trees, helping to soften that area.

10. Dry the work with a hairdryer on a low heat.

11. Brown madder alizarin and neutral tint are mixed, and a No. 6 round brush is used to darken the area at the bottom of the trees on the right.

12. Use the same mix, and the side of a round brush, to add darker foliage and depth to the trees on the left.

13. Now change to a No. 3 rigger brush and add a few fine branches, flicking them in with the same mixture of paint.

14. Add the figures: practise a composition on a piece of scrap paper first. Ensure that the heads of the two taller figures are above the horizon line. This helps to link up the two halves of the painting. Cadmium red is the dominant colour of the left-hand figure, cobalt blue and neutral tint of the centre figure and burnt sienna of the smaller one. All the heads are made from burnt sienna and neutral tint.

15. Do not overwork the figures. The dog is just a brush mark on a lead! Use a neutral tint here.

16. Indicate the telegraph pole using the chisel edge of the flat brush and a touch of neutral tint.

17. The same tint is used with a No. 3 rigger brush to suggest the fence posts on the left.

18. Mix cobalt blue and neutral tint and use a No. 4 round brush for the shadows in the snow at both right and left of the picture.

19. Add some burnt sienna to the foreground to indicate the shapes and shadows along the edge of the footpath and to complement the colourful figures.

20. It is always a good idea to place a mount around the painting before it is completed. This helps to show whether further work is needed.

21. Paint in a few footsteps under and around the figures, using a weak mixture of brown madder alizarin and neutral tint.

22. As a final touch to the figures, add a few shadows on the left of each, using a darker tone of the original colours.

The painting is complete – do not forget to sign it!

A similar subject to the one above, also by Bryan Thatcher, painted with different colours. Try this one – using your own choice of colours.

In each of these paintings, Ray Campbell Smith used a variegated wash to create the effect of a clear sky.

Sunset on the Ouse
Richard Bolton

This dramatic sky was made by applying the clouds — a mix of ultramarine, alizarin crimson and burnt sienna — wet-into-wet on a background wash of raw sienna. The colours mixed on the paper to form the ragged edges. The same colours are echoed on the surface of the water.

Trees

It has been said that if you can paint trees then you can paint landscapes. Well, that may not be quite true, but it certainly helps, as Bryan Thatcher shows in the examples on these two pages.

The problem with painting trees is that we know that there are tens of thousands of leaves on a tree – and we are tempted to try to paint most of them. This is best overcome by half closing your eyes and observing the overall shapes. Keep your brush strokes simple and loose and don't use overpowering greens; it is better to mix more subtle hues.

Note how the trees look lonely! It is sometimes best to link them together by overlapping them as in the example below.

Sap green and burnt sienna have been used here. Running burnt sienna into the wet sap green has encouraged the subtle blending of the two colours. Burnt umber was used for the tree trunks, raw sienna for the foreground, and cobalt blue for the background trees.

Just paint the overall shape of trees, not too much detail.

Bright, warm colours can be used for summer and autumn trees. Here, a group of trees were painted wet-into-wet using burnt sienna, brown madder alizarin, burnt umber, raw sienna and neutral tint.

Bryan Thatcher uses cold colours for winter trees. Here a wet-into-wet mixture of cobalt blue was used to depict winter trees that have retained their foliage.

60

These fir trees are made from just a few simple brush strokes.

A dry brush carrying burnt sienna has been used to depict the outer foliage of this tree. Burnt umber was then run into the damp colour and a little sap green, burnt umber/neutral tint and raw sienna were added in the lower areas of the trunks and grasses.

Burnham Beeches
Bryan Thatcher

Using washes

The tree sketches on this page were painted by Ray Campbell Smith. He advises that the best way of capturing the ragged outlines of trees in full leaf is to hold the brush almost parallel to the paper so that the side rather than the tip produces the image. This technique works best on Rough paper, but is perfectly possible on NOT. The side of the brush comes into contact with the little bumps in the paper's surface but misses the depressions, thus creating the desired broken outline.

The procedure is this: first prepare two washes – the first for the colour of the sunlit foliage, the second for the foliage in shadow. Load the brush with the first wash and apply it, as described, with the side of the brush – concentrate not only on producing the broken outline of the foliage, but also on the overall shape of the tree. When the first wash is complete but still moist, apply the second, deeper-toned wash, wet-into-wet, to the side of the tree away from the source of light and also to the undersides of the branches.

This approach is not quite as easy as it sounds, but with practice you will learn to paint trees convincingly and economically. Avoid making your trees too solid by trying to incorporate some of the sky holes through which sections of branch and trunk are often seen.

Winter trees

Winter trees present rather different problems, though the need to simplify complex forms is just as necessary. Beginners often have difficulty with branches pointing forward or away, and content themselves with painting just the laterals! The only answer here is closer observation and practice. If you study the mass of twiggery at the ends of the branches, the need to simplify becomes obvious. Some painters use a dry-brush technique to capture its effect, others, after the style of Rowland Hilder, prefer to use a pale wash to represent the twigs and the sky beyond. Try both methods and see which suits you best.

A deciduous tree

Stage 1

Stage 2

A conifer

Stage 1

Stage 2

A bare winter tree

Stage 1

Stage 2

Colour

Most ready-mixed greens contain too much blue for foliage use, and many painters therefore prefer to mix their own. You could use raw sienna with a little Winsor blue, or, for a duller effect, Payne's gray, sometimes adding burnt sienna for a little warmth. Always analyse the colour of the trees you are painting and do not accept uncritically the convention that they are just green. Look for the warmer colours – oranges, yellows and browns – and make the most of them. This will not only call attention to colours the casual observer is likely to miss, but will add interest and variety to your work. These warmer colours are most apparent, of course, in the autumn months but hints of them are usually present earlier in the year. If they need a little emphasis or even exaggeration, so be it!

For more distant foliage, cool blues and greys replace the warmer greens. Tonal contrast is greatly reduced or lost altogether, so that a bank of distant trees may well be represented by a flat wash, perhaps of French ultramarine with a little light red. Trees in the middle distance are far enough away for detail to be lost and so also lend themselves to simple, painterly treatment.

Shadows

The shadows in trees demand careful scrutiny. Do not be content with just a darker version of the green you are using for the body of the tree, and look for traces of blue, purple and other colours. Tree trunks, too, repay careful observation, with subtle greys and greens more in evidence than the conventional brown. Study the shapes of the shadows falling on the trunks, and ensure your treatment reinforces their cylindrical form. Remember that trunks are usually in deep shadow as they emerge from under the mass of foliage.

Tea in the Garden
Ray Campbell Smith

Trees in detail

Trees that are supporting elements in a composition can be rendered with a simple, almost flat wash. On the other hand, if a tree is the main subject of a composition, it will require more treatment and detail.

Trees come in all shapes and sizes, and it's a good idea to make lots of sketches of them during the different seasons of the year. Seeing the bare bones of deciduous trees in winter will help you clothe them with foliage. These sketches by William Newton show just a few of the many shapes and textures you can create.

Tree in Winter

A dead tree, or one depicted in winter without its foliage, is best painted from the ground upwards. Even so, you might still need a very light pencil line around its outer shape to show how it will fit into a composition. Exploiting different tones, one branch against another, will help to make a tree into a three-dimensional object.

Oak tree

This old oak tree was painted very rapidly, wet-into-wet, in late summer. The foliage was painted in first then, while these colours were still wet, the dark branches and twigs were run in and allowed to merge slightly. Note how the ground shrubbery contrasts with the pale colours of the lower trunk.

Willow tree

Weeping willows are a joy to paint as they have a good, expansive branch structure and interesting foliage. The bulk of the foliage was painted wet-into-wet, then allowed to dry. The long trailing strands of foliage were then added using the dry-brush technique, dragging the brush strokes vertically downwards.

Walnut tree

Always look for trees with interesting shapes. You do not just want to paint sticks of candyfloss! This ancient walnut tree has an almost hollow trunk and looks rather windswept. Make sketches as often as possible and then add them to a composition when the available trees are not that interesting.

Old Oak Tree

In this demonstration of an old oak tree in a landscape, William Newton uses a combination of techniques – loose free washes, dry-brush work and fine line work with a rigger brush.

What you need

Paints:
  Cobalt blue
  French ultramarine
  Light red
  Raw sienna
  Lemon yellow
Brushes:
  19mm (in) flat
  38mm (1°in) flat
  No. 10 round
  No. 12 round
  No. 1 rigger
Paper:
  Rough, 425gsm (200lb)

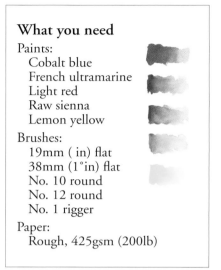

Field sketch. Although this sketch is quite detailed, it is best to transfer the minimum of detail to the watercolour paper – the horizon line, the general outline of the tree and the position of its trunk.

1. Use the 38mm (1°in) flat brush and clean water to wet the paper down to the horizon. Mix a wash of French ultramarine, cobalt blue and a touch of light red, then use the 19mm (in) flat brush to lay in the sky. Make broad strokes across the paper and allow the colour to fade towards the horizon.

2. Add a little light red to the sky mix and continue to lay in the wash, warming the colours as you move downwards.

3. Add a touch of dilute raw sienna to the mix and lay in the final stroke across the horizon.

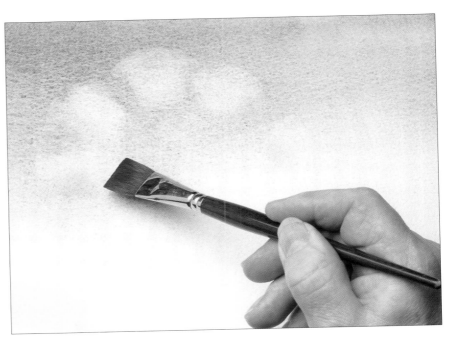

4. Next, start to paint the foliage of the tree. Thoroughly clean the brush and place small areas of raw sienna (mixed with a touch of water) into the still-wet blue sky. You will find that the raw sienna repels the blue and leaves a warm undercolour over which the foliage can be developed. The brush lifts out some of the blue, so rinse it well and load fresh colour for each area.

5. Use the No. 10 round brush and a mix of cobalt blue with a touch of light red to paint in the distant horizon while the paper is still damp.

6. Make up a dryish green mix from French ultramarine and lemon yellow, with touches of raw sienna and water. Use the side of the brush and the dry-brush technique to start building up the foliage.

7. Strengthen the green mix with a little more French ultramarine then, bearing in mind the position of the light source, drop this into the wet foliage to create shadowed areas.

8. Mix a wash of French ultramarine and light red to create a neutral grey and, while the foliage is still wet, use the rigger brush to paint the upper part of the tree trunk and the thicker branches.

10. Using the same mix, and the No. 10 round brush, run colour into the tree trunk. Dilute the tone on the right-hand side to create form.

9. Continue to add more branches, allowing some of the darker colour to run into the greens of the foliage. Remember that branches get progressively thinner towards their tips, so start each stroke with the rigger held down and then gently lift it to the tip.

11. Mix lemon yellow with touches of French ultramarine and raw sienna, then use the No. 12 round brush to lay broad strokes of colour across the foreground area.

12. Mix French ultramarine, lemon yellow and light red, then use a No. 10 round brush and random, short downward strokes to lay in the hedge behind the tree. Vary the tones to create light and shade.

13. Mix French ultramarine with a touch of light red and use the tip of the brush to add the fence posts. Dilute the mix slightly, then add shadows to the trunk and across the grass at the base of the tree.

The finished painting. Cast shadows were added to the trunk of the tree to emphasise the right-to-left light source. Finally, the tip of a rigger brush was used to add a flock of birds in the sky – this complements this simple composition.

Early Morning

This demonstration by Frank Halliday shows how to paint trees without including too much detail. The artist has used a limited palette to help harmonise the picture. The secret of painting these soft moody scenes is to wet the paper before you start to paint; have your colours mixed ready; work quickly; and paint in as much as you can whilst the paper is still slightly damp. Do not work on a wash that is over-saturated with water, as any colour you introduce on top will be dramatically weakened.

1. Sketch in the main outlines with a 4B pencil, then use an old brush and masking fluid to mask out the sun and selected tree trunks.

What you need

Paints:
  Raw sienna
  French ultramarine
  Alizarin crimson
  Burnt umber
Brushes:
  No. 12 round
  No. 6 round
  No. 1 rigger
  Old paint brush
Paper:
  Rough, 640gsm (300lb)
Other materials:
  Masking fluid
  Paper tissue
  4B pencil

3. Form a piece of paper tissue into a point and, while the wash is still wet, lift a little colour from around the sun.

2. Wet the paper. Use a No. 12 round brush to drop in a raw sienna wash over the top part of the sky. Introduce a grey wash of French ultramarine with a little alizarin crimson and burnt umber. Lay in the puddles in the foreground using the same wash.

4. Use the same wash as in step 2 to paint in the trees in the far distance.

5. Blend raw sienna, burnt sienna, and a mix of burnt umber and French ultramarine into and beneath the distant grey trees.

6. Use the same colours, but in stronger tones, to paint in the shrubs in the middle distance.

7. Gently remove the masking fluid by rubbing it with your finger.

8. Use a No. 1 rigger brush with various mixes of the colours already used to suggest distant trees.

9. Add darker details to the trunks of the silver birch trees, then add the branches.

10. Lightly wet the foreground tree trunk. Use a No. 6 round brush and a No. 1 rigger brush to drop in French ultramarine and burnt umber. Do not paint the base of the trunk, as it is bathed in mist.

11. Use a No. 1 rigger brush and French ultramarine to paint in the further branches.

12. Gradually introduce deeper, warmer tones of burnt umber to paint the branches in the middle distance, then the darker foreground ones.

13. Suggest fine twigs at the top of the tree using a No. 12 round brush and French ultramarine mixed with burnt umber. Use weaker washes on the tops of the other trees.

14. Use the same colours but mixed in different proportions to indicate twigs and grass in the foreground, and to suggest a path.

15. Link the foreground to the middle distance by painting in a few tiny trees. Work with a No. 1 rigger brush and the same colours as used in the previous few steps.

The finished painting. There are very few detailed brushstrokes in this project,
which helps to achieve the soft effect.

Country Lane

Trees, bushes, shrubs and all other types of greenery can be suggested using washes. Here, Frank Halliday used the wet-into-wet technique to create a mass of soft green foliage.

1. Apply a flat wash of raw sienna using a No. 12 round brush. Mix up various strengths of green washes using Winsor blue (green shade) with cadmium yellow, and Payne's gray with cadmium lemon. Drop these colours on to the wet wash to create the impression of foliage.

2. Use a No. 6 round brush and a weak mix of Winsor blue (green shade) with a touch of burnt sienna to paint in the distant tree trunks.

3. Paint the path using the same wash as in step 2. Use a No. 12 brush to add the foreground tree trunks and foliage in stronger mixes of the burnt sienna and Winsor blue (green shade).

The finished painting. Foliage can be suggested quite simply, without being painted in great detail. Here, the strength of tones is gradually increased towards the foreground to give a sense of depth (aerial perspective).

Old Oak Door
Jackie Barrass
The foliage in this painting has been treated very simply, concentrating more on the shadows than the foliage itself.

Autumn Fields
Ray Campbell Smith

The wet-into-wet technique has been used for the foliage in this painting to give the impression of autumn mist, and the bluer tones used for the trees on the left create the effect of distance.

Lacework of Branches
Richard Bolton

This painting reproduces in great detail the shapes and patterns created by the bare winter tree.

Opposite
Hoar Frost
Richard Bolton

In this scene, painted by the same artist, a wash is used to suggest the general shape of the trees, and the detail of the branches and twigs is simplified.

Water and Reflections

Painting water is perhaps one of the most daunting challenges for the beginner. However, it need not be too big a stumbling block. As always, the trick is to observe carefully and to paint what you see: a dark area here and a light area there; light tones, half tones and full tones.

Light reflected in smooth water can enliven the dullest landscape when portrayed in clear, fresh washes. It also serves the useful function of linking the sky to the scene below. To capture the full beauty of reflected light, you need to make it appear to shine. This can be done partly by using pale-toned washes and partly by placing deep-toned passages alongside, to provide contrast.

Problems can arise in certain conditions when the breeze fragments the surface into thousands of minute ripples, creating a mass of detail that no watercolour technique can describe without excessive overworking and consequent loss of freshness. The only answer to this problem is to view the reflections through half-closed eyes, so that the tiny details merge to produce a smooth pattern which a wet-into-wet technique can suggest economically and effectively. It sometimes happens that the breeze itself will soften the reflections in this manner, to make your task simpler.

Willow Stream
Ray Campbell Smith

Fishermen's Cottages
Ray Campbell Smith

Speed is all-important when painting wet-into-wet reflections, as the desired effect will be lost if premature drying occurs. It is vital, therefore, to study the colours and tones you need and prepare your washes in advance. Ray Campbell Smith's method is to apply one or more pale washes, approximating to the colour of the reflected sky, to the whole of the water area. He then uses vertical brush strokes to drop in the various reflections, wet-into-wet, using the washes already prepared. A few darker accents, still soft-edged, will complete the picture. This technique is illustrated in the painting opposite of willows by a stream.

If your chosen subject is complicated, anything approaching a mirror image reflection will result in an over-busy painting, with the reflections competing with the scene above instead of complementing it. In such a situation it is best to opt for soft-edged reflections, whatever the conditions.

Hard-edged reflections also need careful study before you put brush to paper. Here again, it is best to begin by applying a pale wash or washes to the whole water area, but then allow drying to take place before putting in the reflections of the objects above. Some simplification is necessary or the reflections can become over-complicated. It sometimes helps to make the whole area of the darker reflections hard-edged while using a wet-into-wet method within the darker area, a technique used in the painting above.

Different types of water

Water appears in an infinite variety of situations, and it serves different purposes within a composition, so there can be no one method of painting it.

One of the challenges of painting water is that, unless the surface is absolutely still, the pattern of the reflections is continually moving and changing. What you must do, after careful study, is to freeze an instant of time in your mind's eye and then paint partly from memory. As with so much in art, this requires careful observation and plenty of practice, but the results will reward the effort.

On these two pages, William Newton shows how he paints various forms of water.

Still water

In very still water, reflections are almost mirror images of the objects behind the water. However, they should have a slightly fuzzy look to them and the reflected colours should be less intense.

Rippled reflections

This boat is moored on water that has a slight ripple on its surface. Note how the reflection of the boat is a little distorted and 'wobbly'. Note also how the light colours of the boat are slightly darker in its reflection.

Puddles

A little artistic licence is often required when painting puddles. You need to place them strategically so that they reflect verticals – in this case, the post and the stern of the barge.

Moving water

Movement in water is perhaps the most difficult subject to capture. Again, observation is the key. In a choppy sea, the tones of each wave appear darker towards the top and lighter in the troughs. Sometimes, white paper can be left to represent the 'white horses' of breaking waves. Compare this sketch with that of the moving water in the waterfall below.

Waterfall

For this type of rushing water, the trick is what you do not paint, rather than what you do paint! In other words, most of the water is just white paper, with just a few softened brush strokes to add reflections as appropriate.

Wet road

The method here is similar to that used for the rippled water. Roads are not perfectly flat, so reflections will be slightly distorted across the surface.

It is worth taking care to ensure that reflected details such as windows, vertical lines and figures, are positioned accurately.

Scottish Loch

In this demonstration of a Scottish loch, Ray Campbell Smith shows how he uses hard-edged reflections to suggest the rippling surface of the water. There is quite a lot to remember when painting ripples! Not only do you have to bear in mind their colour, which must relate to that of the area being reflected, but you have to give your wash an irregular indented edge to represent the ripples.

1. Sketch in the essential elements of the picture. Lay in the main sky area using a 25mm (1in) flat brush and raw sienna with a touch of light red. Use the same colour, but much diluted, for the sunlit area of the clouds. Use a mix of ultramarine and light red for the cloud shadows. Finally, add a wash of ultramarine with just a touch of light red for the blue of the sky. Leave to dry.

What you need

Paints:
  Raw sienna
  Burnt sienna
  Light red
  French ultramarine
  Winsor blue

Brushes:
  25mm (1in) flat
  No. 8 round
  No. 10 round
  No. 12 round

Paper:
  NOT or Rough, 425gsm (200lb) or over – or under 425gsm (200lb) if stretched

Other materials:
  2B pencil

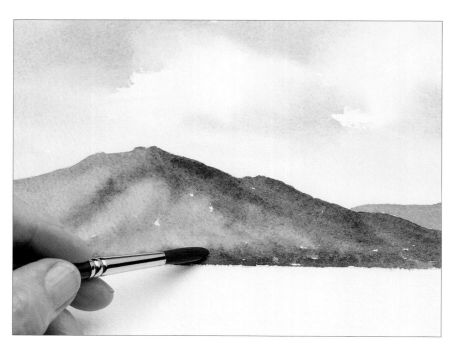

2. Paint in the mountains using a No. 10 round brush. Use raw and burnt sienna for the lighter areas of the main mountain, and ultramarine and light red for its shadows. Leave to dry, then use a lighter version of this last mix for the distant mountains. Add a mix of burnt and raw sienna with a touch of Winsor blue for the trees along the distant shoreline. Apply this wet-into-wet, then leave to dry.

3. Paint in the middle distance trees using the side of a No. 10 round brush and varying proportions of raw sienna, burnt sienna and Winsor blue. Add shadow with a No. 8 round brush. Leave to dry.

4. Use a 25mm (1in) flat brush to paint in the water. Lay in washes with vertical strokes, in colours which roughly correspond to the sky area above. Leave to dry.

5. Paint in the reflections in the water using all three round brushes. Use raw sienna, burnt sienna and Winsor blue for the reflections of the sunny parts of the mountains. Use French ultramarine and light red for the reflections of the shadows on the mountains. Leave a pale, untouched strip to suggest a band of wind-ruffled water – this serves the useful purpose of separating the distant scene from its reflection.

The finished painting

Farm Pond

On perfectly still days reflections are virtually mirror images, while the presence of wind causes rippling. Slight breezes frequently produce a softer effect. Here, the conditions are such that the reflections in the pond are soft-edged and Ray Campbell Smith demonstrates how to use the wet-into-wet technique to obtain the desired effect.

1. Sketch in the essential elements of the picture. Lay in the sky using the same colours and brushes as shown in step 1 of the Scottish Loch project on page 84. Leave to dry.

2. Paint in the roofs of the buildings using various combinations of light red and burnt sienna, each mixed with a touch of French ultramarine. Use a No. 10 round brush to put in the main body of colour and a No. 8 round brush to add detailing. Use raw sienna and a touch of Winsor blue to suggest moss; burnt sienna for the brick building; and burnt sienna and French ultramarine for the wooden building. Leave to dry then put in a few texturing strokes, following the slope of the roofs. Leave to dry.

3. Paint in the trees and hedges with a No. 10 round brush, using varying combinations and strengths of raw sienna, burnt sienna and Winsor blue. Use a No. 8 round brush to lay in the shadows. Leave to dry.

4. Lay in the distant hills using a No. 8 round brush and French ultramarine mixed with light red. Paint in the foreground grass using a No. 12 round brush and a broken wash of raw sienna mixed with a little Winsor blue. Add a little Payne's gray and burnt sienna, then paint in the shadowed areas and the gate with a No. 8 round brush. Leave to dry.

5. Use a No. 10 round brush to paint over the entire pond with the colours used for the sky, to give a pale background. Add vertical strokes, wet-into-wet, for the reflections of the trees and buildings. Finally, add a few dark accents.

The finished painting

Chub Stream

Living next to a river has given artist Richard Bolton a lot of experience of painting water. He likes painting water scenes on warm summer evenings, before the sun goes down, when its golden hues spread across the water and mix with the deep shadows of the trees on the river bank. He also enjoys winter scenes, and the challenge of trying to capture the shades of grey of the ice as it spreads across the surface.

The subject for this demonstration is a little stream overhung by a large tree that creates an attractive arch. The one problem presented by this scene is the depth of tone – the foliage is very dark – and there is a danger of overworking the paint and creating a dull image. To avoid this, Richard Bolton works quickly and repeatedly returns to the palette to make fresh colour mixes. Later, he defines the foliage in more detail by overpainting a variety of other colours.

The depth of tone of the foliage is repeated in the reflections in the stream, but here the challenge is to create the impression of movement by depicting the ripples in the water.

What you need

Paints:
  Cerulean blue
  Ultramarine
  Raw sienna
  Burnt sienna
  Viridian
  Cadmium orange
  Burnt umber
  Alizarin crimson
  Indian red
  Naples yellow
  Chinese white
Brushes:
  No. 6 round
  Old split brush
  Small, stiff oil-painting brush
  Old paint brush
Paper:
  NOT, 190gsm (90lb),
    stretched on a board
Other materials:
  2B pencil
  Masking fluid
  Razor blade
  Eraser
  Paper tissue

In this reference photograph, it is difficult to make out the distant bridge. The bridge is the focal point of this scene, so the artist painted it more clearly and made its arches more visible.

1. Sketch in the outlines of the main elements of the scene. Use masking fluid and an old brush to mask all the swans. Mix a wash of cerulean blue with a touch of burnt sienna, then use a No. 6 round brush to paint the sky.

88

2. Mix ultramarine with a touch of burnt sienna, then wash in the foreground water, blending it with the still-damp colour of the sky. Paint around the highlighted areas of the boat.

3. Work down to the bottom of the painting, gradually increasing the intensity of colour. Note the effect of granulation (above). If you like this effect, leave the painting to dry face up. However, if you do not want a granular effect, turn the painting board upside-down and dry the painting, face down (right). Note how the granulation has been reduced.

Never throw old brushes away. They are very good for the split-brush technique

4. Mix raw sienna and ultramarine with a touch of burnt sienna, then use an old brush and the split-brush technique to develop the foliage. Add a tiny touch of viridian to vary the tone. A word of warning about viridian – use too much and the painting will look 'chocolate boxy'.

5. Use a weak wash of ultramarine and a No. 6 round brush to paint in the distant trees behind the bridge. Soften the top of these trees and the bottom of the fir tree with clear water.

6. Add more raw sienna to the wash and develop the large tree (centre and right of the painting). Vary the tone to create shape and form. Go back over the foliage with darker tones to create the texture of leaves in the foliage. Use burnt sienna to develop shadows under the right-hand trees and below the house.

When mixing colours in his palette, Richard Bolton likes to have lots of tones available around the edge of the mix. This picture shows the mix of greens used to paint the foliage in step 6.

7. Use a mix of Naples yellow and alizarin crimson to define the bridge. Vary the tones with touches of Chinese white to create texture. Use the Naples yellow and alizarin crimson mix to wash in reflections of the bridge, leaving a highlight between the bridge and its reflection.

8. Use a mix of burnt umber, ultramarine and a touch of Indian red to paint the reflections of the trees.

9. Use the same mix to block in the dark arches under the bridge. Continue to build up reflections using the washes in the palette.

10. Add a touch of raw sienna to a wash of burnt sienna, then paint the brickwork of the wall on the bank of the river. Dilute the wash slightly, then work the reflections in the water.

11. Use a wash of alizarin crimson, Naples yellow and ultramarine to paint the gable end of the house. Dilute the wash, add more Naples yellow, then paint the side of the house. Add more alizarin crimson and ultramarine, then paint the roof. Leave to dry.

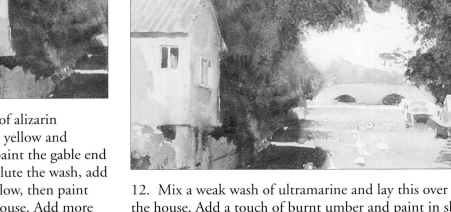

12. Mix a weak wash of ultramarine and lay this over the gable end of the house. Add a touch of burnt umber and paint in shadows and windows. Remember to leave highlights. Use the same mix to develop the boat. Use all the colours to define shape in the building and bridge.

13. Use a razor blade to scratch a highlight across the water, then go over the area with an eraser.

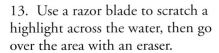

14. Remove the masking fluid from the swans. If colour has penetrated on to the masked area, use a stiff oil-painting brush and clear water to scrub out the colour. Dab off excess moisture with paper tissue.

15. Mix a weak wash of cadmium orange, then paint the middle distant and foreground swans and their reflections. Use ultramarine and alizarin crimson for shadows on all swans. Paint the beaks with cadmium orange.

Opposite
The finished painting. The artist went back over the whole painting, adding points of interest: the suggestion of tiles on the roof; more texture on the walls; and some detail on the distant swans. He overpainted highlights on the foliage using the split-brush technique and a mix of Naples yellow with touches of viridian and Chinese white. He also developed the reflections to create more movement in the water.

92

Fishing Village
Ray Campbell Smith

*Hard-edged reflections are used in this painting
to suggest the rippled surface of the water.*

Opposite
Minchin Forestry Recreational Park, Taiwan
Richard Bolton

*The deep colours in a lake can be difficult to
achieve without them becoming dull and
overworked. For this scene, Richard Bolton
applied a number of washes to build up the
dark rich tones, but he had to be careful to
avoid forming hard edges or causing the
previous wash to run.*

Buildings

Cottages and farms are an integral part of the rural scene and should receive just as much thought and consideration as any other part of the landscape. Indeed, their geometric form requires rather more forethought than that of natural features such as trees and foliage. For example, a building seen head-on rarely has the same appeal as a more oblique view, with some walls in light and some in shadow. Similarly, a group of farm buildings strung out in a straight line makes a far less appealing subject than the same buildings seen from a different viewpoint, so that they overlap and form a cohesive and more interesting group. The buildings in the painting below by Ray Campbell Smith are an example of this sort of treatment. These are considerations you should always bear in mind when planning a composition.

Old buildings have a special attraction and by their very age become almost part of the natural scene. You should aim to emphasise their venerable character, perhaps by stressing their wayward lines and by exaggerating any signs of weather-staining. They present the same sort of detail problems as any other element in the landscape – when they are close enough to enable us to see every brick and tile individually, just how much detail should we put in? The answer has to be just sufficient to identify the nature of the building materials – a few small areas of

Farm Lane
Ray Campbell Smith

Roofscape, La Roque
Ray Campbell Smith

brickwork or a few random stones will provide sufficient information and the rest can safely be left to the imagination. The sketch shown here is an example of this sort of treatment.

Buildings are often part of a rural landscape, but they obviously predominate in cities, towns and villages. Such scenes have just as much right to be described as landscapes and often offer excellent subject matter for the perceptive artist. You should at all times aim to keep an open and enquiring mind and respond to artistic stimuli whenever you encounter them. You will then see possibilities in the most unlikely places, often on your own doorstep. Stanley Spencer and Lowry drew their inspiration from their own environments, one with his Thames-side settings, the other with his interpretations of industrial Lancashire.

It sometimes pays to look for an unusual angle or viewpoint, to bring a touch of originality to a conventional or even mundane scene. The painting above by Ray Campbell Smith is an example of this, and here the high vantage point facilitated the development of the pattern of pantiled roofs.

Look for tonal contrast wherever it exists and, within reason, move the constituent parts of the scene so that lights and darks are placed side by side. Notice the important part played by the shadows in the painting by Ray Campbell Smith featured here.

Those parts of buildings usually seen against the sky, such as tall gables and chimneys, always look dark by contrast with their pale background and should be painted in correspondingly deep tones. Windows deserve more care than they frequently receive and should not be rendered simply as uniform grey oblongs. Sometimes there is a glimpse of curtain, sometimes there is reflected light and sometimes there is just the dark interior – and often a mixture of all three. Ring the changes to produce variety. However, as with other subjects, you should not aim for minute attention to detail – windows, like any other architectural features, can be effectively suggested by a loose technique.

Evening in Venice
Ray Campbell Smith
Tonal contrast is created in this painting by placing the dark shadows and bright sunlit areas side by side.

Chapel at Last Light

This simple composition by Jackie Barrass shows an old building in a landscape. The demonstration will teach you to lay a graded wash, and you can also practise using masking fluid to protect highlights. Use plenty of water during the initial stage so that the whole surface remains wet. You will soon gain confidence in handling broad washes and working quickly across the entire paper surface.

A photograph of the scene on which Jackie Barrass based her painting.

What you need

Paints:
  Burnt umber
  Cobalt blue
  Cobalt violet
  Raw sienna
  French ultramarine
  Permanent rose
Brushes:
  25mm (1in) flat
  No. 8 round
  No. 14 round
  No. 1 rigger
  Old paint brush
Paper:
  Rough, 300gsm (140lb)
Other materials:
  2B pencil
  Masking fluid
  The end of a small brush
    or a stick

1. Sketch in the main components of the landscape using a 2B pencil.

2. Apply masking fluid to the roof and front of the building, the window, the front of the wall and the gate. Use the end of a small brush, an old brush or a stick to apply it. Leave to dry.

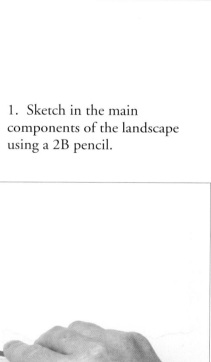

100

3. Mix cobalt blue with a touch of permanent rose, then use the flat brush to work a stroke of it at the top of the painting. Now work a band of raw sienna and allow the colours to blend.

4. Continue working down the painting, applying bands of permanent rose, then cobalt violet, raw sienna, burnt umber and finally cobalt blue.

5. Use a No. 8 round brush to add touches of raw sienna here and there to introduce more light to the wash.

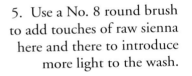

6. Build up the trees and hedges on the horizon by adding in French ultramarine.

7. Add touches of French ultramarine and permanent rose to the top of the wall, then leave to dry.

8. Paint in the bell tower and the gable end of the building using French ultramarine mixed with permanent rose. Then use the same mix to define the low wall in front of the building.

9. While the paint is still wet, use the rigger to drop in touches of burnt umber on the gable end of the building and the low wall.

10. Apply French ultramarine under the eaves of the building. Leave to dry.

11. Use a No. 14 round brush to add a wash of permanent rose over the foreground of the painting.

12. Complete the foreground area by adding touches of burnt umber, then leave to dry.

13. Use a No. 8 round brush and a mix of cobalt violet and cobalt blue to define the distant trees. Leave to dry.

14. Remove the masking fluid.

Note *You can use a putty eraser to remove final traces of masking fluid.*

15. Use a No. 8 round brush to work a wash of raw sienna over all the areas that were masked. Strengthen the mix for the windows in the gable end of the building.

16. While the paint is still wet, add touches of permanent rose to the roof and side of the building, and to the low wall. Leave to dry.

17. Add final details to the bell tower, windows, eaves, gate and wall using a No. 1 rigger and a mix of French ultramarine and permanent rose.

The finished painting. Light has a dramatic effect on a painting, and tonal contrast can be used to add interest to a composition including a building. You could add further drama to this subject by darkening the foreground or, alternatively, change the mood completely by painting the view with the sun behind you, thereby lighting the gable-end against a much darker sky.

Washday
Jackie Barrass
This painting has a light airy feel.
The artist's attention was caught by
the architectural detail of the temple
shown up by the strong light.
Masking fluid was used in the initial
stages to preserve highlights.

Passage of Light
Jackie Barrass

Once again, light has been used to dramatise this painting of a building. The shaft of sunlight made an interesting shape in this doorway and set up lovely areas of reflected light in the shadows. Darks have been strengthened in the foreground to give the impression of a shaded, narrow alleyway.

Opposite
Greek Stairway in Shadow
Jackie Barrass

Simplification of the subject and the immediacy of the watercolour medium help to capture this scene of a typical Greek building.

Farm House
Richard Bolton

Richard Bolton uses a variety of watercolour techniques to create the detail of buildings. For this farm house, he rubbed a little candle wax on the areas of stonework, then brushed over this with ultramarine and a little burnt sienna to create a speckled texture.

Rooftops can be quite difficult to paint convincingly. Do not try to paint every single tile; patches of detail here and there are all you need – the eye tends to fill in the rest. Burnt sienna is the perfect colour for rusty iron sheeting, but here the artist added a little yellow to lighten some areas, and red to provide richer colours in others.

Stone Wall
Richard Bolton

Candle wax was rubbed over the wall area to create the effect of stonework in this painting. Then masking fluid was applied to individual stones where the light catches the edge of them.

The colours, ultramarine, Naples yellow and burnt sienna, were applied to a background wetted with clear water. While the paint was still wet, the dark gaps between the stones were added, and the paint was allowed to mix with the background colours.

Empty Window
Richard Bolton

Windows and doors provide excellent subjects to paint, and their geometric shapes blend well against irregular stonework.

To make this subject work as a painting, the artist softened the outer edges with clear water. The resultant vignette helps the composition by drawing the eye to the centre of the painting. Try not to overload this type of painting with detail, and allow colours and textures to mix naturally on the paper.

Flowers

Watercolour is the ideal medium for capturing the freshness and vibrancy of flowers. As with the other subjects covered in this book, there are many different ways of painting them, depending on the effect you hope to achieve.

One method is to paint a misty background and then pull flowers out of it, deepening around and behind each flower instead of overpainting it. Some artists prefer to paint straight on to dry white paper, and to add a little background later. Wendy Tait, who painted the pictures on these two pages, prefers to begin with a gentle background in the colour range of the flowers she is using, and to then build her painting from there, finishing with the tiny darks that give the all-important contrasts.

As with other subjects, good painting depends on good observation, but a successful painting can often depend on what is suggested but not painted in detail. The imagination will supply the eye with the necessary information if led in the right direction. Don't try to paint botanical illustrations, but rather suggest the feeling of the flowers, the season, even the smell. A painting that achieves these things can really appeal to the emotions of the viewer.

One of the challenges of flower painting is deciding when a painting is complete. Deciding this is quite a milestone as it is so easy to take things a little too far and become 'fiddly'.

It is worth noting that in flower painting, warm or cool tones can be used to create a feeling of climate rather than direct botanical illustration. Pale mixes of lemons, blues and greens make a cool painting, while pinks and reds create warmth. To warm up a painting, you can begin with the same palette as for a cool scene, and simply change the proportions of mixes, for example, adding tiny amounts of orange to pinks, to create warmer reds.

Summer Meadows
Wendy Tait

This painting was painted on site, and the artist has tried to capture the fresh looseness of the flowers and grasses in the field.

Primroses and Campanulas
Wendy Tait

These blue and violet campanulas contrast with the pale yellow of the primroses. Note the misty blue background flowers painted on wet paper, that carry the blue tones right through the painting.

Daffodils and Primroses
Wendy Tait

Cool colours are used in these pale flowers early in the season. Their freshness is contrasted with a bluey violet mix in the background, with added strength behind the central flowers. The colours used are cobalt blue deep, Winsor lemon, new gamboge, Winsor violet, permanent rose and a green mixed from Winsor lemon, Payne's gray and cobalt blue.

Sweet Peas
Wendy Tait

This painting uses mainly the same colours as the one above, but the artist has changed the balance towards warmth by creating more pinks and reds and by adding more violet to the background. She used cobalt blue deep, Winsor violet, quinacridone magenta, permanent rose, Winsor orange and a basic green mix.

113

Techniques

There are four illustrations of painting terms here, but any one of them can be applied to each of the examples of flower painting. The compositions shown, by Wendy Tait, all contain elements of counterchange, negative painting, lost and found edges and aerial perspective. Although these sound like complicated terms, they describe simple things – in fact, you are probably already achieving what is covered here, without thinking about it!

Lost and found edges

This is a term used to describe how soft and sharp lines can both be used to define elements in a painting. The lilac blossom here sometimes emerges with a sharp (found) edge, against a background of leaf or shadow, or it appears to be indistinct, and its edge becomes lost.

Counterchange

In simple terms, counterchange means light against dark, dark against light. It is used to emphasise elements of the painting. In this example of cherry blossom, the pale pink blossom has been painted against darker pink blossom and the very dark background is placed behind light areas. Also note the little dark buds against the pale background.

114

Negative painting

The way to create a delicate flower is to paint the background, not the flower. This is called negative painting and it can be used to great effect. It is a way of suggesting form by painting the negative rather than the positive image that you see. For example, in this loose painting of foxgloves and daisies, you can see how the white daisies are created by the little dark shapes around them – these have been carefully painted to suggest leaves and half-seen flowers. Another example can be seen in the small areas between the stems as they cross each other.

Aerial perspective

Aerial perspective is used in landscapes to show how objects close to you are larger and stronger in colour, tone and detail, than those further away. It is used on a smaller scale with flowers too, to make sure the eye is drawn first of all to the three main roses. Note the detail and warmer tones used on the large roses in the foreground and compare them to the background roses and leaves.

Note Successful painting is often about timing. The exact moment to deepen a slightly drying wash (usually when the shine goes off the paper) can only be learned by trial and error. Only many hours of experimentation can teach you this kind of technique!

115

Composing your painting

Once you have decided what you want to paint, set up your subject (or position yourself if you are outside) so that you have a good light source coming clearly from one direction. You will find it easier to paint if you can pinpoint exactly whether the subject is backlit or sidelit. If you can avoid a flat, overhead light, you will help yourself considerably.

Divide your paper into imaginary thirds vertically and horizontally, to create nine sections. Your main flower, or group of flowers should cross one of these intersections and be just off-centre. It is best to keep them low in the painting. Begin with these and work outwards with softer, smaller flowers, keeping strong tones and contrasts towards the central group.

direction of light

Pink Roses
Wendy Tait

Wendy Tait divides her painting into nine roughly equal sections. The main flower(s), will be located roughly in the middle section, just off centre, as shown by the circled area.

117

Daffodils and Catkins

This first project is a simple one painted straight on to dry white paper, and it includes just a trace of a background. The tones gradually deepen as the painting progresses; each time a deeper tone is used, a smaller area is covered. It is important to keep your tones very pale in the initial stages of the painting so as not to lose the light – you can always darken them later if you feel you need to.

It is best to work from real flowers. If they are in a vase, as these daffodils are, you can turn them as you work, to get the angle of each flower that you want. Paint them approximately life size, on an A3 (16˝ x 11 in) or A4 (11 x 8˝in) paper block.

Before you begin, prepare some colour mixes in your palette. In this demonstration, Wendy Tait used a basic green mix of Payne's gray and Winsor lemon; a blue mix of cobalt blue deep with a touch of violet; a yellow mix of Winsor lemon and new gamboge, and a brown mix of raw sienna with a touch of Winsor violet.

Begin with a piece of paper larger than you think you will need. This allows for 'headroom' as your painting grows.

What you need

Paints:
    Winsor lemon,
    Cobalt blue deep
    Winsor orange
    New gamboge
    Winsor violet
    Raw sienna
    Payne's gray

Brushes:
    No. 10 or 12 round
    Hake

Paper:
    NOT

1. Use the yellow mix to paint in the centre of the daffodil then add a little of the basic green mix to the centre. Deepen this green mix with a little cobalt blue deep then use this to paint the shadows, avoiding outlining the petals if possible.

2. Darken the centre with the blue-green mix. Add more new gamboge to the yellow mix to create a stronger colour, then use this to define the flower centre. Create a few shadows using a little raw sienna.

118

3. Paint in the trumpet of the second flower with the stronger yellow mix. Paint in two petals with the pale yellow mix.

4. Add details to the petals using a touch of the green mix. Paint in the centre of the trumpet using deeper tones of the yellow with a touch of raw sienna. Add clean water to the paint to dilute the colours towards the trumpet edge.

5. Paint in the third flower using the paler yellow mix and add the green mix to the base. Paint in the more deeply shadowed petals using warmer tones. Dilute the colour towards the edges, as in the previous step.

6. Use a warmer golden tone to paint in the trumpet. Use paler tones to strengthen the outline of the petals. Add raw sienna to the stronger yellow mix and define the crinkles at the edge of the trumpet. Use the same golden tones with a touch of violet to add the caul. Paint in the deep tone on the shadow side, then add water to the colour on the paper to dilute it slightly. Lift off a little colour with your brush to suggest light coming from above.

8. Paint in the catkins using raw sienna and Winsor violet added to the green mix. Leave to dry thoroughly.

7. Use the basic green mix, with a touch of cobalt blue deep, to paint in the stems. Leave areas of white where they are highlighted. Add the leaves, blending and diluting the colour where the leaves turn.

9. Wet the white paper behind the flowers using the round brush, then use the hake brush to wet the large area right to the edge of your paper. Use the round brush to drop in a mix of cobalt blue deep with a touch of violet, making sure the colour runs and deepens behind the flower.

Note *Work from the outer edge of the petals in towards the centre or more deeply-toned area to avoid hard edges. Sometimes, you may find it helps to turn your paper as you work.*

*The finished painting. Adding just a
little background colour right at the end,
pulls out the central daffodil. Note that
the trumpet is slightly off-centre so that
the stamens give an idea of the shape.*

Roses

Wendy Tait, who painted the rose studies on this page, says that the key to painting roses is to relax – it does not matter if you are on the 'wrong row' of petals – only you will know. With practice, you will find your own way to paint these marvellous flowers, but here are a few tips worth remembering to set you on your way:

- Rose thorns always curve downwards

- The veins are rarely seen the whole length of the leaf

- The shine on the leaves of roses (and ivy and holly) is blue in shade

- When painting a red rose, paint in quite a pale colour to begin with, then paint in the deep tones later

- When painting a pale rose, remember that a little paint goes a long, long way

Rose studies

These three roses are painted loosely from photographs – this is a good way of painting roses in the winter! Do not try too hard to make an exact copy of the photograph, but use the time as a practice exercise only, to help you prepare for painting from life later in the year. Note the cool tones on the outer petals of the pink rose, and the warm tones in the centre of the white rose. The centres of all the roses have been painted without too much detail, leaving a little to the imagination.

Garden Roses
Wendy Tait

A basic green mix was used then gold and raw sienna were added to warm the greens and give them the deep tones. Notice how the intense darks only cover very small areas.

Backlit Lily

Positive and negative shapes are used to portray this well-lit lily by Jackie Barrass. The paint is applied using a controlled wet-into-wet technique. Let the medium do the work and try not to overpaint the flower head so that it becomes laboured and dull.

A photograph of the lilies on which Jackie Barrass based her painting.

What you need

Paints:
    Aureolin
    Burnt sienna
    Cobalt violet
    Permanent magenta
    Pthalo blue
    Winsor red

Brushes:
    No. 8 round
    No. 14 round
    No. 1 rigger
    Old paint brush

Paper:
    Rough, 300gsm (140lb)

Other materials:
    2B pencil
    Masking fluid
    The end of a small brush
      or a stick

This sketch was drawn from life, then used as the composition for this demonstration.

1. Sketch in the main elements of the painting. Use the end of a paint brush to apply masking fluid to the stamens and pistils.

2. Roughly wet the area around the lily flower head using a No. 14 round brush. Drop in aureolin, pthalo blue and permanent magenta onto the wet areas. Allow the colours to run into each other.

3. While still wet, use a No. 8 round brush and the same colours as in the previous step to further define the edges of the petals. Leave to dry.

4. Remove some of the pencil marks around the edges of the petals then dampen the middle of the petals, leaving the very outer edges dry. Use a No. 8 round brush to drag in almost undiluted permanent magenta in the centre of each petal. This will soften off over the pre-dampened paper.

5. Drop in a small amount of pthalo blue at the base of some of the petals to give impact.

6. Use a No. 1 rigger and permanent magenta mixed with a touch of Winsor red to add spots around the base of the petals. Leave to dry.

7. Remove the masking fluid from the stamens and pistils, then paint the base of the stamens using aureolin and a No. 8 round brush. Leave to dry.

8. Paint in the pistils using burnt sienna and a No. 1 rigger brush. Leave to dry.

9. Use a No. 8 round brush and a mix of pthalo blue and burnt sienna to lightly define the stems, buds and leaves.

10. Use cobalt violet followed by pthalo blue to introduce shadow to the petals.

*The finished painting.
Star Gazer lilies really
glow when they are
back-lit and thrown
into sharp focus against
a dark background –
this is the effect conveyed
in this painting.*

131

Irises

Flower studies provide the opportunity to experiment. Richard Bolton likes to focus on one or two flower heads, and depict them in detail against a soft, contrasting background, as in this demonstration. Irises are ideal for this type of treatment. They are very sculptural, and the strong, bold outlines of their petals and foliage work very well against a soft, seemingly out-of-focus background.

Before starting to work on the background, Richard Bolton applies masking fluid to all the foreground detail. This allows him to work loosely and quickly over the whole area of the paper. The wet-into-wet technique is used to work splashes of colour into the background, allowing the colours to blend together on the paper. Then salt is added to the wet colours to create other interesting effects.

The most important factor about flowers is their freshness, so do not overwork the colours or techniques.

What you need

Paints:
  Cerulean blue
  Prussian blue
  Alizarin crimson
  Gamboge
  Cadmium orange
  Viridian
  Ultramarine
  Burnt sienna
  Dioxazine violet
Brushes:
  No. 6 round
  No. 14 round
  Old paint brush
Paper:
  NOT, 190gsm (90lb),
    stretched on a board
Other materials:
  2B pencil
  Masking fluid
  Table salt
  Razor blade
  Soft eraser
  Hairdryer

You can paint from photographs of blooms that will not be around for long, but it can be very pleasant sitting in the garden working from life.

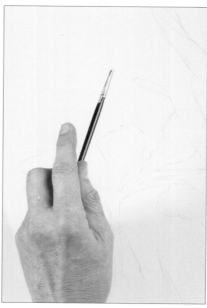

1. Use masking fluid and an old brush to outline all the flower petals, stems and leaves. Flick spots of masking fluid randomly over the background area.

2. Use a No. 14 round brush and clear water to wet parts of the background area.

3. Mix a wash of cerulean blue, then paint this randomly across the top part of the background.

4. Mix a wash of Prussian blue with a touch of alizarin crimson, then paint this across the middle parts of the background.

5. Add more alizarin crimson to the wash as you near the bottom of the painting.

6. Dilute the wash, then use a No. 6 round brush to lay in a spike of foliage, wet into wet. Splatter spots of cadmium orange, wet-into-wet, randomly over the background colours.

Salt will continue to work while the paint is wet. You can stop the effect at any time by drying it with a hairdryer.

7. Sprinkle salt randomly over the wet paint. The effect starts almost immediately and will continue to develop all the while the paint is wet.

8. When you are happy with the salt effect, dry the painting with a hairdryer – watch out for unwanted hard edges forming.

9. When the paper is dry, start to remove the masking fluid with a soft eraser...

...then pull off the larger pieces with your finger.

This wash of gamboge, ultramarine and viridian still shows traces of the individual colours.

10. Mix a wash of gamboge and a touch of ultramarine, then paint in the leaves and stems. Add a spot of viridian to the wash as you work down the leaves.

11. Add more ultramarine to the wash and start to develop the tone and shape of the foliage. Use the tip of the brush to define the edges of the foliage. At this stage, take care not to overwork the picture, as much of its charm relies on the speed and handling of the paint.

135

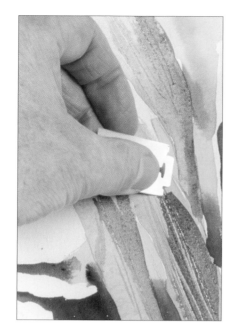

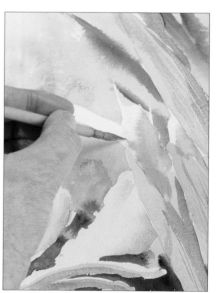

12. Leave the paint to dry slightly, then use the end of a razor blade to scratch fine lines into the dark colours and reveal the paler tones beneath.

13. Mix ultramarine with a touch of burnt sienna and tiny spots of gamboge. Paint the shadowed areas of the white petals, then soften some edges with clear water to make them merge into the white of the paper.

14. Use gamboge and a small round brush to start building up colour on the petals. Soften each area with clear water. Add some shadows using a wash of ultramarine and viridian.

15. Mix dioxazine violet with touches of ultramarine and gamboge, then add tone and shape to the hues.

The finished painting

Irises
Richard Bolton

This painting is a variation of the demonstration on pages 132–137.

As in the demonstration, Richard Bolton used masking fluid to mask out the foreground detail while he worked on the background. He wetted the paper with clear water, then applied very fluid mixes of cerulean blue and Prussian blue. Gamboge was dropped, wet-into-wet, on to the surface and allowed to spread out into the blues. A brush charged with ox gall was dragged over the surface and salt scattered into the wet paint to add interest and textures.

The white of the flower petals works well against the darker background and only a little shading of ultramarine, with a touch of burnt sienna, was needed to complete the picture.

Poppies
Richard Bolton

The colour of these flower heads needs to be bright and vibrant, so the artist used scarlet lake, which retains its brightness when dry. The whole painting was executed with speed and energy to give it a lively, spontaneous quality.

Masking fluid was used extensively to create the many highlights on the flower heads and background details. These flashes of white paper are crucial and really bring this painting to life.

Daisies
Jackie Barrass

The artist used a limited palette of only three colours to give a quick, spontaneous response to the crisp freshness of these flowers.

Primroses, Pansies and Heather
Wendy Tait
This simple little painting illustrates how well pale
primroses show up when just a little foliage and
background are dropped in behind them.

Spring Flowers
Wendy Tait

142

Index